FRENCH
in 10 minutes a day®

by **Kristine Kershul**, M.A., University of California, Santa Barbara
adapted by Jan Fisher Brousseau

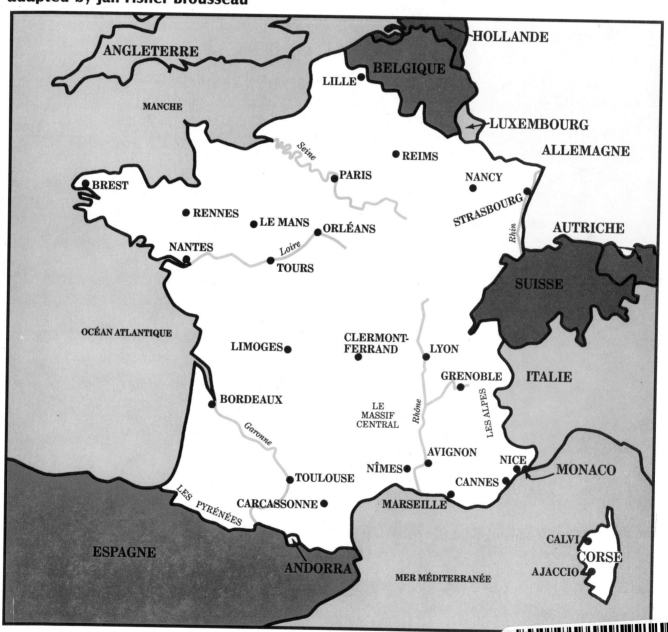

Bilingual Books Inc.
511 Eastlake Avenue E., Seattle, WA 98109
Tel: (206) 340-4422   Fax: (206) 340-9816

W9-BYK-870

Fifth printing October 1995

Copyright © 1992, 1988, 1981, Bilingual Books Inc., Seattle, WA 98109. Second edition. All rights reserved. ISBN 0-944502-57-1.

L'alphabet

(ahl-fah-bay)

Many French letters sound the same as in English, but some French letters are pronounced or written differently. To learn the French sounds of these letters, write each example in the space provided in addition to saying the word many times. After you practice the word see if you can locate it on the map.

French letter	English sound	Example	(Write it here)
a	ah	**P**aris (pah-ree)	
au/eau	oh/oe	Bord**eau**x (bore-doe)	
c (before a,o,u)	k	**C**ar**c**assonne (kar-kah-sohn)	
c (before e,i,y)	s	Ni**c**e (nees)	*Nice*
ç	s	Alen**ç**on (ah-lah[n]-soh[n])	
ch	sh	**Ch**ampagne (shah[n]-pahn-yuh)	
e	uh	L**e** Mans (luh mah[n])	
é	ay	Orl**é**ans (or-lay-ah[n])	
ei	eh	S**ei**ne (sehn)	
è/ê	e (as in let)	Norv**è**ge (nor-vezh)	
g (before a,o,u)	g	**G**aronne (gar-own)	
g (before e,i,y)	zh (as in leisure)	**G**ironde (zhee-rohnd)	
gn	ny (as in onion)	Avi**gn**on (ah-veen-yoh[n])	
i	ee	L**i**lle (leel)	
j	zh	Le **J**ura (luh zhew-rah)	
o	oh	Lim**o**ges (lee-mohzh)	
qu	k	**Qu**ébec (kay-bek)	
r	(slightly rolled)	**R**ennes (ren)	
s (between vowels)	z	Toulou**s**e (too-looz)	
u	eu/ue	T**u**nisie (tew-nee-zee)	
x (varies)	gz	E**x**eter (eg-zuh-tare)	
	ks	Lu**x**embourg (lewk-sum-boor)	
	s	Au**x**erre (oh-sair)	*Auxerre*
y	ee	Nan**cy** (nah[n]-see)	

NASAL VOWEL SOUNDS

am, an, em, en	ah[n] (taunt nasalized)	**An**gleterre (ah[n]-gluh-tare)	
im, in, aim, ain, ein, eim	a[n] (than nasalized)	R**eim**s (ra[n]s)	
om, on	oh[n] (don't nasalized)	Toul**on** (too-loh[n])	
um, un	uh[n] (fun nasalized)	Mel**un** (mel-uh[n])	

2

When you arrive in **France** *(frah⁽ⁿ⁾-s)* or **Québec,** *(kay-bek)* the very first thing you will need to do is to ask questions — "Where is the train station?" "Where can I exchange money?" "Where *(oo)* (**où**) is the lavatory?" "**Où** is the restaurant?" "**Où** do I catch a taxi?" "**Où** is a good hotel?" "**Où** is my luggage?" — and the list goes on and on for the entire length of your visit. In French, there are SEVEN KEY QUESTION WORDS to learn. For example, the seven key question words will help you to find out exactly what you are ordering in a restaurant before you order it — and not after the surprise (or shock!) arrives. Take a few minutes to study and practice saying the seven basic question words listed below. Notice that "what" and "who" are only differentiated by one letter, so be sure not to confuse them. Then cover the French words with your hand and fill in each of the blanks with the matching **mot** *(mow)* **français.** *(frah⁽ⁿ⁾-say)*
word   French

1.	**OÙ** *(oo)*	= WHERE	_____
2.	**QUI** *(key)*	= WHO	_____
3.	**QUE/QU'** *(kuh)*	= WHAT	_____
4.	**POURQUOI** *(poor-kwah)*	= WHY	_____
5.	**QUAND** *(kah⁽ⁿ⁾)*	= WHEN	*quand, quand, quand*
6.	**COMMENT** *(ko-mah⁽ⁿ⁾)*	= HOW	_____
7.	**COMBIEN** *(kohm-bee-yen)*	= HOW MUCH	_____

Now test yourself to see if you can really keep these **mots** *(mow)* *words* straight in your mind. Draw lines between the French **et** *(ay)* *and* English equivalents below.

why	**qui**
what	**que**
who	**où**
how	**combien**
where	**quand**
when	**pourquoi**
how much	**comment**

Examine the following questions containing these **mots** *(mow)*. Practice the sentences out loud many times **et** *(ay)* *and* then quiz yourself by filling in the blanks below with the correct question **mot**.

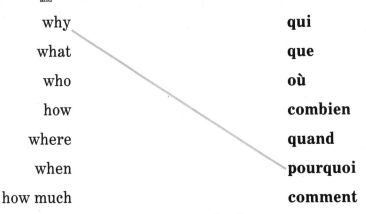

(oo) (ay) (luh) (tay-lay-phone)
Où est le téléphone?
Where is the telephone?

(key) (ess)
Qui est-ce?
Who is it?

(kohm-bee-yen) (ess)
Combien est-ce?
How much is it?

(kah⁽ⁿ⁾) (luh) (tra⁽ⁿ⁾) (ah-reev-teel)
Quand le train arrive-t-il?
When the train does it arrive?

(kess) (key) (suh)(pahss)
Qu'est-ce qui se passe?
What's happening?

(ko-mah⁽ⁿ⁾) (ay) (lah) (sah-lahd)
Comment est la salade?
How is the salad?

(kess) (kuh) (say)
Qu'est-ce que c'est?
What is it?

(poor-kwah) (luh) (tra⁽ⁿ⁾) (nah-reev-teel) (pah)
Pourquoi le train n'arrive-t-il pas?
Why doesn't it arrive?

1. _*Comment*_ est la salade?

2. _____ est-ce?

3. _____ est-ce qui se passe?

4. _____ est le téléphone?

5. _____ le train n'arrive-t-il pas?

6. _____ est-ce?

7. _____ le train arrive-t-il?

8. _____ est-ce que c'est?

Où will be your most used question **mot,** so let's concentrate on it. **Répétez** *(ray-pay-tay)* *repeat* the following French sentences aloud. Then write out each sentence without looking at the **exemple.** *(eg-zahm-pluh)* If you don't succeed on the first try, don't give up. Just practice each sentence until you are able to do it easily. Don't forget that **"qu"** is pronounced like "k" and **"est-ce"** like "ess."

4 Also, in French, the letter **"h"** is silent and **"th"** is pronounced like "t."

Où $sont^{(soh^{(n)})}$ $\begin{cases} \text{les cabinets?} \\ \text{les toilettes?} \end{cases}$ *(lay) (kah-bee-nay)* *(twah-let)*

Où est le taxi? *(ay) (luh) (tahx-ee)*

Où est l'autobus? *(ay) (low-toe-boos)*

_____ *Où est le taxi?* _____

Où est le restaurant? *(ay) (luh) (res-toe-rah^{(n)})*

Où est la banque? *(lah) (bah^{(n)}k)*

Où est l'hôtel? *(ay) (low-tell)*

_____ _____ _____

Oui, many of the **mots** which look like **anglais** are also **français.** Since **français et** *(wee)* *(mow)* *(ah^{(n)}-glay)* *(frah^{(n)}-say)* *(ay)*

yes — English — French

anglais share many words, your work here **est** simpler. You will be amazed at the *(ay)*

is

number of **mots** which are **identiques** (or almost **identiques**). Of course, they do not *(ee-dah^{(n)}-teak)*

identical

always sound the same when spoken by a French person, but the **similarité** will *(see-mee-lar-ee-tay)*

similarity

certainly surprise you. Listed below are five "free" **mots** beginning with "A" to

help you get started. Be sure to say each **mot** aloud **et** then write out the **mot français** *(ay)* *(frah^{(n)}-say)*

in the blank to the right.

☑ **l'accident** *(lack-see-dah^{(n)})* . . . . accident _____
☑ **l'addition** *(lah-dee-see-oh^{(n)})* . . . . the bill in a restaurant _____
☑ **l'admission** *(lahd-mee-see-oh^{(n)})* . . . . admission _____
☑ **l'adresse** *(lah-dress)* . . . . address *l'adresse, l'adresse*
☑ **aidez-moi!** *(ay-day-mwah)* . . . . aid me! help me! _____

Free **mots** like these will appear at the bottom of the following pages in a yellow color

band. They are easy --- enjoy them!

Step 2 — "the," "a," "some"

All of these words mean "the" in **français**:

(luh) **le**	*(lah)* **la**	**l'**	*(lay)* **les**

(gar-soh⁽ⁿ⁾) **le garçon:** the boy
(fee-yah) **la fille:** the girl
(lome) **l'homme:** the man

(gar-soh⁽ⁿ⁾) **les garçons:** the boys
(fee-yah) **les filles:** the girls
(lay-zome) **les hommes:** the men

These two words mean "a" or "an":

(uh⁽ⁿ⁾) **un**	*(ewn)* **une**

(tra⁽ⁿ⁾) **un train:** a train
(uh-nome) **un homme:** a man
(fahm) **une femme:** a woman
(sah-lahd) **une salade:** a salad

These words mean "some":

(dew) **du**	*(duh lah)* **de la**	*(duh)* **de l'**	*(day)* **des**

(soo-kruh) **du sucre:** some sugar
(moo-tard) **de la moutarde:** some mustard
(la⁽ⁿ⁾-tay-ray) **de l'intérêt:** some interest
(day-sair) **des desserts:** some desserts

Le français *(frah⁽ⁿ⁾-say)* (French) has multiple **mots** for "the," "a," and "some," but there **est** *(ay)* (is) no need to worry about it. Just make a choice **et** *(ay)* remember to use one of these **mots** when you mean "the," "a" **ou** *(oo)* (or) "some."

Step 3 — Les Choses

(lay) *(showz)* **Les Choses** (things)

Before you proceed **avec** *(ah-vek)* (with) this step, situate yourself comfortably in your living room. Now look around you. Can you name the things which you see in this **pièce** *(pea-ess)* (room) in **français?**

Probably you can guess **la lampe** *(lahmp)* and maybe even **la chaise** *(shehz)*. Let's learn the rest of them.

After practicing these **mots** out loud, write them in the blanks below **et** *(ay)* on the next page.

(tah-blow) **le tableau** = the picture _____le tableau, le tableau_____

(plah-foh⁽ⁿ⁾) **le plafond** = the ceiling _____

☑ **l'alcool** *(lahl-kohl)* . . . . alcohol _____
☐ **les Alpes** *(lay zahlp)* . . . . the Alps _____
☐ **américain** *(ah-may-ree-ka⁽ⁿ⁾)* . . . . American _____
☐ **l'animal** *(lah-nee-mawl)* . . . . animal _____
☐ **l'appartement** *(lah-par-teh-mah⁽ⁿ⁾)* . . . . . apartment _____

le coin *(kwa(n))* = the corner _____

la fenêtre *(fuh-net-ruh)* = the window *la fenêtre, la fenêtre, la fenêtre*

la lampe *(lahmp)* = the lamp _____

la lumière *(lew-mee-air)* = the light _____

le canapé *(kah-nah-pay)* = the sofa _____

la chaise *(shehz)* = the chair _____

le tapis *(tah-pee)* = the carpet _____

la table *(tahb-luh)* = the table _____

la porte *(port)* = the door _____

la pendule *(pah(n)-dewl)* = the clock _____

le rideau *(ree-doe)* = the curtain _____

le mur *(mewr)* = the wall _____

You will **notice** that the correct form of **le, la ou les** *(oo)* is given **avec** *(ah-vek)* each noun. This is for [with] your information — just remember to use one of them. Now open your book to the first page **avec** the stick-on labels. Peel off the first 14 labels **et** *(ay)* proceed around the **pièce,** *(pea-ess)* [room] labeling these items in your home. This will help to increase your French **mot** power easily. Don't forget to say **le mot** as you attach each label.

Now ask yourself, **"Où est le tableau?"** *(luh)(tah-blow)* **et** point at it while you answer, **"Voilà** *(vwah-lah)* [there is] **le tableau."** Continue on down the **liste** *(least)* [list] until you feel comfortable with these new mots. Say, **"Où est le plafond?"** *(plah-foh(n))* Then **répondez,** *(ray-poh(n)-day)* [respond] **"Voilà le plafond,"** *(luh)* and so on. When you can identify all the items on the **liste,** *(least)* [least] you will be ready to move on.

Now, starting on the next page, let's learn some basic parts of the house.

☐ **l'appétit** *(lah-pay-tee)* .... appetite _____
☐ **l'arrêt** *(lah-ray)* .... stop, arrest _____
☐ **l'arrivée** *(lah-ree-vay)* .... arrival _____
☐ **l'attention** *(lah-tah(n)-see-oh(n))* .... attention _____
☐ **l'auteur** *(low-tur)* .... author _____

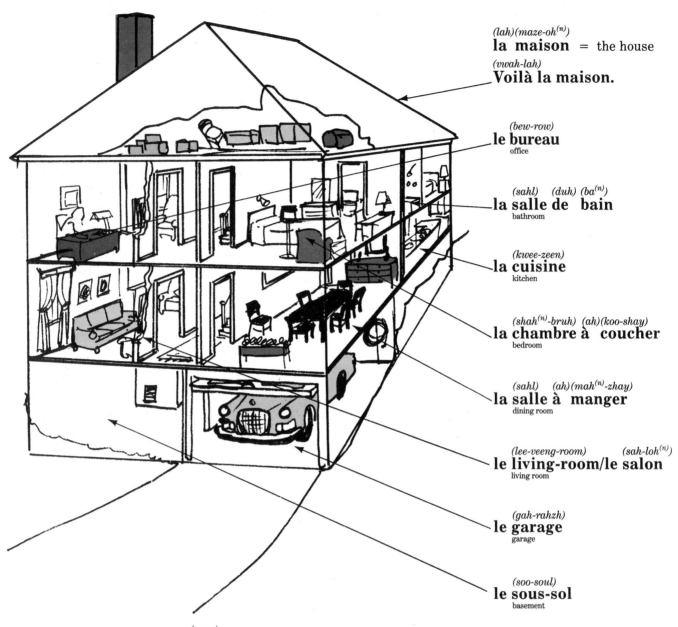

(lah)(maze-oh$^{(n)}$)
la maison = the house
(vwah-lah)
Voilà la maison.

(bew-row)
le bureau
office

(sahl) (duh) (ba$^{(n)}$)
la salle de bain
bathroom

(kwee-zeen)
la cuisine
kitchen

(shah$^{(n)}$-bruh) (ah)(koo-shay)
la chambre à coucher
bedroom

(sahl) (ah)(mah$^{(n)}$-zhay)
la salle à manger
dining room

(lee-veeng-room) (sah-loh$^{(n)}$)
le living-room/le salon
living room

(gah-rahzh)
le garage
garage

(soo-soul)
le sous-sol
basement

While learning these new *(mow)* **mots** let's not forget
words

(low-toe) (vwah-tewr)
l'auto/la voiture

(bee-see-klet)
la bicyclette

(shee-ya$^{(n)}$)
le chien

le chien, le chien

_____   _____

☐ **le balcon** *(bahl-koh$^{(n)}$)* . . . . balcony
☐ **le ballon** *(bah-loh$^{(n)}$)* . . . . balloon, big ball
☐ **la banane** *(bah-nahn)* . . . . banana
☐ **le banc** *(bah$^{(n)}$)* . . . . bench
☐ **la banque** *(bah$^{(n)}$k)* . . . . bank

8

(shah)
le chat
cat

(zhar-da$^{(n)}$)
le jardin
garden

(koo-ree-ay)
le courrier
mail

le jardin, le jardin

(bwaht) (oh) (let-ruh)
la boîte aux letters
mail box

(fluhr)
les fleurs
flowers

(so-net)
la sonnette
door bell

Peel off the next set of labels *(ay)* **et** wander through your *(maze-oh$^{(n)}$)* **maison** learning these new *(mow)* **mots.**

Granted, it will be somewhat difficult to label your **chien, chat ou fleurs,** but use your

(ee-mah-zhee-nah-see-oh$^{(n)}$)
imagination.

Again, practice by asking yourself, <u>**"Où est le jardin?"**</u> *(ray-poh$^{(n)}$-day)* et **répondez,** <u>**"Voilà le jardin."**</u>

Où est

☐ **le bifteck** *(beef-tek)* . . . . beefsteak _____
☐ **le biscuit** *(bee-skwee)* . . . . cookie _____
☐ **la bouteille** *(boo-tay)* . . . . bottle _____
☐ **bref** *(brehf)* . . . . brief, short _____
☐ **brillant** *(bree-yah$^{(n)}$)* . . . . brilliant, sparkling _____

9

Step 4

Un, deux, trois *(uh^n) (duh) (twah)*
one   two   three

This is part of a little rhyme that **les enfants** *(ah^n-fah^n)* **français récitent:** *(ray-seat)*
children   recite

(uh^n) (duh) (twah) **Un, deux, trois** one two three	*(zhuh) (vay) (dah^n) (lay) (bwah)* **je vais dans les bois** I go into the woods
(kah-truh) (sank) (sees) **Quatre, cinq, six** four five six	*(kuh-year) (day) (sir-eez)* **cueillir des cerises.** to pick some cherries

For some reason, numbers are not the easiest thing to learn, but just remember how important they are in everyday **conversation.** *(koh^n-vair-sah-see-oh^n)* How could you tell someone your phone number, your address or your hotel room if you had no numbers? And think of how difficult it would be if you could not understand the time, the price of an apple or the correct bus to take. When practicing the **nombres** *(nome-bruh)* below, notice the **similarités** *(see-mee-lar-ee-tay)* between numbers   similarities **quatre** *(kah-truh)* (4) and **quatorze** *(kah-torz)* (14), **sept** *(set)* (7) and **dix-sept** *(deez-set)* (17) **et** so on.

0	*(zay-row)* **zéro**		0	_____
1	*(uh^n)* **un**	11 *(oh^nz)* **onze**	1	_____
2	*(duh)* **deux**	12 *(dues)* **douze**	2	_____
3	*(twah)* **trois**	13 *(trehz)* **treize**	3	_____
4	*(kah-truh)* **quatre**	14 *(kah-torz)* **quatorze**	4	*quatre, quatre, quatre*
5	*(sank)* **cinq**	15 *(ka^nz)* **quinze**	5	_____
6	*(sees)* **six**	16 *(says)* **seize**	6	_____
7	*(set)* **sept**	17 *(deez-set)* **dix-sept**	7	_____
8	*(wheat)* **huit**	18 *(deez-wheat)* **dix-huit**	8	_____
9	*(nuf)* **neuf**	19 *(deez-nuf)* **dix-neuf**	9	_____
10	*(dees)* **dix**	20 *(va^n)* **vingt**	10	_____

☐ **la capitale** *(kah-pee-tahl)* .... capital
☐ **la cathédrale** *(kah-tay-drahl)* .... cathedral
☐ **le cendrier** *(sah^n-dree-ay)* .... ashtray (cinders)
☐ **le centre** *(sah^n-truh)* .... center
☐ **le champagne** *(shah^n-pahn-yuh)* .... champagne

_____
_____
_____
_____
_____

(ew-tee-lee-zay) *(nome-bruh)*
Utilisez these **nombres** on a daily basis.   Count to yourself **en français** *(ah$^{(n)}$)* when you brush
use

your teeth, exercise, **ou** *(oo)* commute to work.   Now fill in the following blanks according to
or

the **nombres** given in parentheses.

Note: This is a good time to start learning these two important phrases.

(zhuh) *(voo-dray)* **Je voudrais**	=	I would like _____
(new) *(voo-dree-oh$^{(n)}$)* **Nous voudrions**	=	we would like _____

(zhuh) *(voo-dray)*
Je voudrais _____ (15)

(fuh-yuh) *(duh)* *(pah-pee-ay)*
feuilles de papier.
sheets   of   paper

(kohm-bee-yen)
Combien? _____ (15)

Je voudrais _____ (10)

(kart) *(pohs-tall)*
cartes postales.
postcards

Combien? _____ (10)

Je voudrais _____ (11)

(ta$^{(n)}$-bruh-post)
timbres-poste.
stamps

Combien? _____ (11)

Je voudrais _____ (8)

(lee-truh) *(day-sah$^{(n)}$-s)*
litres d'essence.
liters   of gas

Combien? *huit* (8)

Je voudrais _____ (1)

(vair) *(duh)* *(zhew)* *(door-ah$^{(n)}$zh)*
verre de jus d'orange.
glass   of   orange juice

Combien? _____ (1)

(new) *(voo-dree-oh$^{(n)}$)*
Nous voudrions _____ (3)

(tahs) *(duh)* *(tay)*
tasses de thé.
cups   of   tea

Combien? _____ (3)

Nous voudrions _____ (4)

(tee-kay) *(doe-toe-boos)*
tickets d'autobus.
bus tickets

Combien? _____ (4)

Nous voudrions *deux* (2)

(bee-air)
bières.
beers

Combien? _____ (2)

Je voudrais _____ (12)

(uh) *(fray)*
oeufs frais.
eggs   fresh

Combien? _____ (12)

Nous voudrions _____ (6)

(lee-vruh) *(duh)* *(vee-ah$^{(n)}$d)*
livres de viande.
pounds   of   meat

Combien? _____ (6)

Nous voudrions _____ (5)

(vair) *(doe)*
verres d'eau.
glasses   of water

Combien? _____ (5)

Je voudrais _____ (7)

(vair) *(duh)* *(va$^{(n)}$)*
verres de vin.
glasses   of   wine

Combien? _____ (7)

Nous voudrions _____ (9)

(lee-vruh) *(duh)* *(buhr)*
livres de beurre.
pounds   of   butter

Combien? _____ (9)

□ **le changement** *(shah$^{(n)}$-zhuh-mah$^{(n)}$)* . . . . change _____
□ **le chèque** *(shek)* . . . . bank check _____
□ **le chocolat** *(show-ko-lah)* . . . . chocolate _____
□ **le coiffeur** *(kwah-fur)* . . . . hairdresser _____
□ **la communication** *(ko-mew-nee-kah-see-oh$^{(n)}$)* . . communication _____

Now see if you can translate the following thoughts into **français.** **Les réponses** *(lay) (ray-poh(n)s)* are
at the bottom of the **page.** *(pahzh)*

 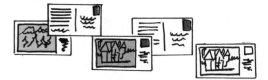

1. I would like seven postcards.

_____

2. I would like one beer. _____ *Je voudrais une bière.*

3. We would like two glasses of water.

_____

4. We would like three bus tickets.

_____

Review **les nombres** 1 **à** 20 **et** answer the following **questions** *(kehs-tee-oh(n))* aloud, **et** then write the
réponses *(ray-poh(n)s)* in the blank spaces to the right.

Combien de tables y *(kohm-bee-yen) (duh) (tahb-luh) (ee)*
a-t-il ici? *(ah-teel) (ee-see)*
there   here

_____

Combien de lampes y *(lahmp) (ee)*
a-t-il ici? *(ah-teel) (ee-see)*
there   here

cinq, cinq

Combien de chaises y a-t-il ici? *(shehz)*

_____

12

Combien de pendules y *(duh) (pah(n)-dewl) (ee)*
a-t-il ici? *(ah-teel)*

_____

Combien de fenêtres y a-t-il ici? *(fuh-net-ruh)*

une, une _____

Combien de personnes y *(pear-sohn)*
a-t-il ici?

_____

Combien d'hommes y *(dome)*
a-t-il ici?

_____

Combien de femmes y *(fahm)*
a-t-il ici?

_____

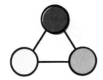

Les Couleurs *(lay) (koo-luhr)*
colors

Step 5

Les couleurs sont the same **en France et au Québec** as **en Amérique**—they just have *(soh(n))* *(ah(n)) (frah(n)-s) (oh) (kay-bek) (ah(n)) (nah-may-reek)*
are in in

different **noms.** You can easily recognize **violet** as violet and **bleu** as blue. So when *(noh(n))* *(vee-oh-lay)* *(bluh)*
names

you are invited to someone's **maison et** you want to bring flowers, you will be able to order *(maze-oh(n))*
house

the **couleur correcte** of flowers. (Contrary to American custom, **en Europe les fleurs** *(ko-rekt)* *(ah(n)) (nuh-rope) (fluhr)*

rouges, et particularly **les roses rouges,** are only exchanged between lovers!) Let's *(roozh)* *(rose)*
red

learn the basic **couleurs.** Once you have read through **la liste** on the next **page,** cover *(koo-luhr)* *(least)* *(pahzh)*

the **français avec** your **main, et** practice writing out the **français** next to the **anglais.** *(ma(n))*
with hand

Notice the **similarités** between **les mots en français et en anglais.** *(see-mee-lar-ee-tay)* *(ah(n)) (frah(n)-say) (ah(n)) (nah(n)-glay)*

☐ **la compagnie** *(koh(n)-pahn-yee)* . . . . company _____
☐ **le/la concierge** *(koh(n)-see-airzh)* . . . . doorkeeper _____
☐ **la conversation** *(koh(n)-vair-sah-see-oh(n))* . . . conversation _____
☐ **le cousin** *(koo-za(n))* . . . . cousin (male) _____
☐ **la cousine** *(koo-zeen)* . . . . cousin (female) _____

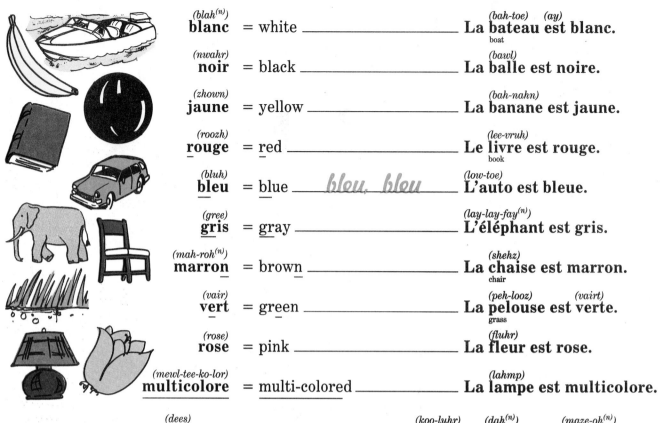

(blah⁽ⁿ⁾)
blanc = white _____
(bah-toe) *(ay)*
La bateau est blanc.
boat

(nwahr)
noir = black _____
(bawl)
La balle est noire.

(zhown)
jaune = yellow _____
(bah-nahn)
La banane est jaune.

(roozh)
rouge = <u>r</u>ed _____
(lee-vruh)
Le livre est rouge.
book

(bluh)
bleu = <u>bl</u>ue ___*bleu, bleu*___
(low-toe)
L'auto est bleue.

(gree)
<u>gr</u>is = <u>gr</u>ay _____
(lay-lay-fay⁽ⁿ⁾)
L'éléphant est gris.

(mah-roh⁽ⁿ⁾)
marron = <u>br</u>own _____
(shehz)
La chaise est marron.
chair

(vair)
<u>v</u>ert = <u>gr</u>een _____
(peh-looz) *(vairt)*
La pelouse est verte.
grass

(rose)
rose = pink _____
(fluhr)
La fleur est rose.

(mewl-tee-ko-lor)
<u>**multicolore**</u> = <u>multi-colored</u> _____
(lahmp)
La lampe est multicolore.

(dees)
Now peel off the next **dix** labels **et** proceed to label these
(koo-luhr) *(dah⁽ⁿ⁾)* *(maze-oh⁽ⁿ⁾)*
couleurs dans your **maison.**
in

Now let's practice using these **mots.**

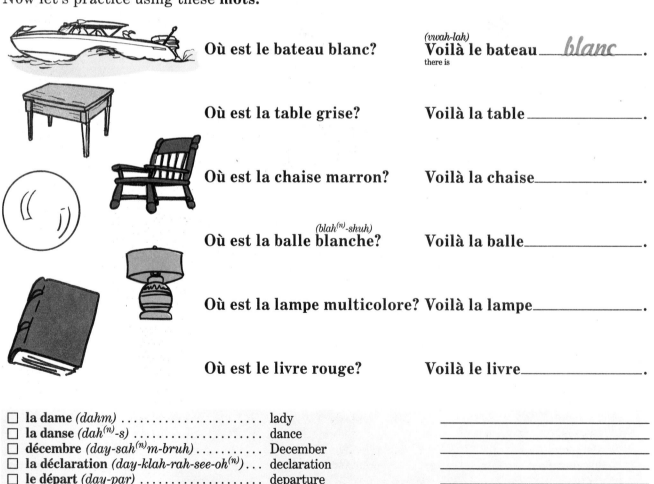

Où est le bateau blanc?
(vwah-lah)
Voilà le bateau ___*blanc*___.
there is

Où est la table grise?
Voilà la table _____.

Où est la chaise marron?
Voilà la chaise_____.

(blah⁽ⁿ⁾-shuh)
Où est la balle blanche?
Voilà la balle_____.

Où est la lampe multicolore? **Voilà** la lampe_____.

Où est le livre rouge?
Voilà le livre_____.

☐ **la dame** *(dahm)* . . . . lady _____
☐ **la danse** *(dah⁽ⁿ⁾-s)* . . . . dance _____
☐ **décembre** *(day-sah⁽ⁿ⁾m-bruh)* . . . . December _____
☐ **la déclaration** *(day-klah-rah-see-oh⁽ⁿ⁾)* . . . declaration _____
14 ☐ **le départ** *(day-par)* . . . . departure _____

Où est la porte verte? *(vairt)*   **Voilà la porte** _____ .

Où est la maison rose?   **Voilà la maison** _____ .

Où est la banane jaune?   **Voilà la banane** _____ .

Note: **En français,** *(ah^{(n)}) (frah^{(n)}-say)* the **verbe** *(vairb)* for "to have" **est "avoir."** *(ah-vwahr)*

j'ai *(zhay)* = I have _____   **nous avons** *(new) (zah-voh^{(n)})* = we have _____

Let's review **je** *(zhuh)* **voudrais** *(voo-dray)* **et nous** *(new)* **voudrions** *(voo-dree-oh^{(n)})* **et learn avoir** *(ah-vwahr)*. **Répétez** *(ray-pay-tay)* each sentence out loud.
I   would like   we   would like   to have

Je voudrais un *(voo-dray)* **verre** *(zuh^{(n)}) (vair)* **de** *(duh)* **bière.** *(bee-air)*   **J'ai un verre de bière.** *(zhay)*

Nous voudrions *(voo-dree-oh^{(n)})* **deux** *(duh)* **verres de vin.** *(va^{(n)})*   **Nous avons deux verres de vin.** *(zah-voh^{(n)})*

Je voudrais un verre d'eau. *(doe)*   **Nous avons une maison.** *(zewn)*

Nous voudrions une salade. *(zewn) (sah-lahd)*   **J'ai une maison en Amérique.** *(ah^{(n)}) (nah-may-reek)*

Nous voudrions avoir une auto. *(zah-vwahr) (oh-toe)*   **J'ai une auto.** *(oh-toe)*

Nous voudrions avoir une auto en Europe.   **Nous avons une auto en Europe.** *(ah^{(n)}) (nuh-rope)*
(ah^{(n)}) (nuh-rope)

Now fill in the following blanks **avec** the **forme correcte** *(form) (ko-rekt)* of "avoir" **ou** *(oo)* "vouloir." *(voo-lwahr)*
or

_____ **trois autos.**
(we   have)

_____ **deux tickets d'autobus.**
(we   would   like)

_____ **un tableau.**
(I   have)

_____ **sept cartes postales.**
(I   would   like)

☐ **déjà** *(day-zhah)* . . . . already   _____
  — déjà vu *(day-zhah vew)* . . . . already seen   _____
☐ **le désir** *(day-zeer)* . . . . desire   _____
☐ **la distance** *(dee-stah^{(n)}-s)* . . . . distance   _____
☐ **le docteur** *(doke-tur)* . . . . doctor   _____   15

Voilà a quick review of the **couleurs** *(koo-luhr)*. Draw lines between **les mots français et les** *(lay) (mow) (frah⁽ⁿ⁾-say)*

couleurs correctes *(ko-rekt)*. On your mark, get set, *GO!*

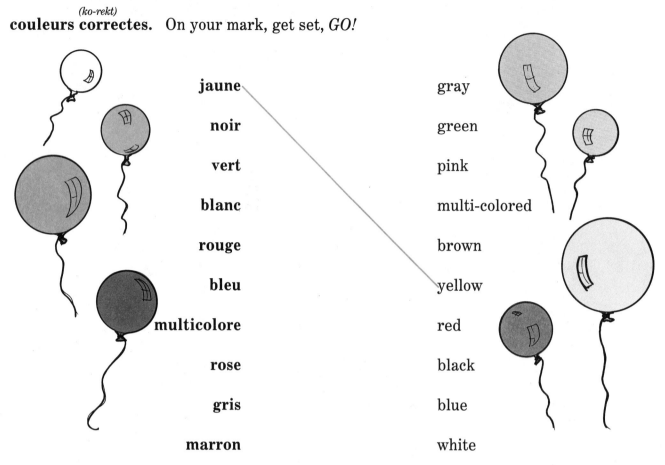

jaune — yellow

noir — gray

vert — green

blanc — pink

rouge — multi-colored

bleu — brown

multicolore — red

rose — black

gris — blue

marron — white

Where to place the accent in French need never be a problem. **Les mots français** *(lay) (frah⁽ⁿ⁾-say)* are

always accented on the last syllable. It's easy!

☐ **l'économie** *(lay-koh-noh-mee)* .... economy _____
☐ **l'entrée** *(lah⁽ⁿ⁾-tray)* .... entry _____
☐ **est** *(est)* .... east _____
☐ **l'état** *(lay-tah)* .... state _____

— **Les États-Unis d'Amérique** *(lay-zay-tah-zoo-nee dah-may-reek)* The United States of America

Step 6

L'Argent
(lar-zhah(n))
money

Before starting this Step, go back **et** review Step 4. Make sure you can count to **vingt** *(va(n))*

without looking back at **le livre.** *(lee-vruh)* Let's learn the larger **nombres** *(nome-bruh)* now, so if something costs

more than 20 **F** *(frah(n))* you will know exactly **combien** *(kohm-bee-yen)* it costs. After practicing aloud **les nombres**

français 10 à 100 below, write these **nombres** in the blanks provided. Again, notice the

similarités *(see-mee-lahr-ee-tay)* between **nombres** such as **quatre** (4), *(kah-truh)* **quatorze** (14) *(kah-torz)* and **quarante** (40). *(kah-rah(n)t)*

10	**dix** *(dees)*	(quatre + six = dix)	10 *dix, dix*
20	**vingt** *(va(n))*	(deux = 2)	20 ___
30	**trente** *(trah(n)t)*	(<u>tro</u>is = 3)	30 ___
40	**quarante** *(kah-rah(n)t)*	(<u>qua</u>tre = 4)	40 ___
50	**cinquante** *(sang-kah(n)t)*	(<u>cin</u>q = 5)	50 ___
60	**soixante** *(swah-sah(n)t)*	(<u>six</u> = 6)	60 ___
70	**soixante-dix** (60+10) *(swah-sah(n)t-dees)*	(sept = 7)	70 ___
80	**quatre-vingts** (4x20) *(kah-truh-va(n))*	(huit = 8)	80 ___
90	**quatre-vingt-dix** (4x20+10) *(kah-truh-va(n)-dees)*	(neuf = 9)	90 ___
100	**cent** *(sah(n))*		100 ___
1000	**mille** *(meel)*		1000 ___

Now take a logical guess. **Comment** *(ko-mah(n))* would you write (**et** say) the following? **Les**

réponses *(ray-poh(n)s)* **sont** at the bottom of **la page.** *(lah) (pahzh)*
are

400 ___   600 ___

2000 ___   5300 ___

RÉPONSES

RÉPONSES

5300 = **cinq mille trois cents**   2000 = **deux mille**
600 = **six cents**   400 = **quatre cents**

17

The unit of currency **en France est le franc français,** abbreviated **F.** Bills are
called **billets** *(bee-ay)* **et** coins are called **monnaie** *(mo-nay).* Just as **un** *(uh(n))* **dollar américain** *(doe-lahr) (ah-may-ree-ka(n))* can be
broken down into 100 pennies, **un franc français** *(frah(n))* can be broken down into 100 **centimes** *(sah(n)-teem).*
A coin is called **une pièce de monnaie** *(ewn) (pea-ess) (mo-nay)* **et** bills can also be referred to as **papier-monnaie** *(pah-pee-ay mo-nay).*
Let's learn the various kinds of **billets** *(bee-ay)* **et monnaie** *(mo-nay).* Always be sure to practice each
mot out loud. You might want to exchange some money **maintenant** *(ma(n)-tuh-nah(n))* now so that you can
familiaize yourself **avec** the various types of **argent** *(ar-zhah(n))* money**.**

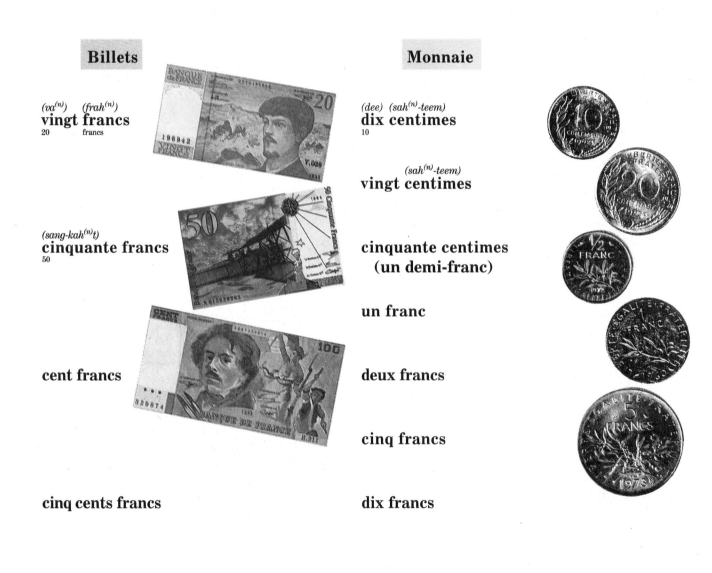

Billets	**Monnaie**
vingt francs *(va(n)) (frah(n))* 20 francs	**dix centimes** *(dee) (sah(n)-teem)* 10
	vingt centimes *(sah(n)-teem)*
cinquante francs *(sang-kah(n)t)* 50	**cinquante centimes (un demi-franc)**
	un franc
cent francs	**deux francs**
	cinq francs
cinq cents francs	**dix francs**

☐ **la fatigue** *(fah-teeg)*	fatigue, tiredness	_____
— **je suis fatigué** *(zhuh swee fah-tee-gay)*	I am tired	_____
☐ **la fête** *(feht)*	feast, festival	_____
☐ **le festival** *(feh-stee-vahl)*	festival	_____
☐ **le film** *(feelm)*	film	_____

Review **les nombres dix** through **mille** again.   **Maintenant,** *(ma[n]-tuh-nah[n])* *now* how do you say "twenty-two"

(oo) **ou** "fifty-three" *(ah[n])* **en français?**   You basically put **les nombres** together in a logical

sequence, for example, 78 (60 + 18) = **soixante-dix-huit.**   See if you can say **et** write out

les nombres on this **page.**   **Les réponses** *(soh[n])* **sont** at the bottom of **la page.**

a. 25 = _____ (20 + 5)	b. 36 = _____ (30 + 6)
c. 47 = _____ (40 + 7)	d. 93 = _____ (4 x 20 + 13)
e. 84 = _____ (4 x 20 + 4)	f. 68 = *soixante-huit* (60 + 8)
g. 51 = _____ (50 + 1)	h. 72 = _____ (60 + 12)

Notice that for 21, 31, 41, 51, 61 and 71 you will put **et** between the two numbers.   To ask

what something costs **en français,** one asks, *(kohm-bee-yen) (ess-kuh) (sah) (koot)* **"Combien est-ce que ça coûte?"**

(ma[n]-tuh-nah[n]) **Maintenant** answer the following questions based on **les nombres** in parentheses.

1. *(kohm-bee-yen) (ess-kuh) (sah) (koot)* **Combien est-ce que ça coûte?** how much   does   it   cost   *(sah) (koot)* **Ça coûte** _____ **francs.** it   costs   (10)

2. **Combien est-ce que ça coûte?**   **Ça coûte** _____ **francs.** (20)

3. **Combien coûte le** *(lee-vruh)* **livre?** how much   costs   **Ça coûte** _____ **francs.** (17)

4. **Combien coûte l'** *(low-toe)* **auto?**   **Ça coûte** *deux mille* **francs.** (2000)

5. **Combien coûte le** *(feelm)* **film?**   **Ça coûte** _____ **francs.** (5)

6. **Combien coûte la** *(shah[n]-bruh)* **chambre?**   **Ça coûte** _____ **francs.** (24)

7. **Combien coûte le** *(tah-blow)* **tableau?**   **Ça coûte** _____ **francs.** (923)

Step 7

(oh-zhoor-dwee) *(duh-ma$^{(n)}$)* *(ee-air)*
Aujourd'hui, demain et hier
today   tomorrow   yesterday

(kah-lah$^{(n)}$-dree-ay) **Le calendrier** calendar

(suh-men) *(ah)* *(zhoor)* **Une semaine a sept jours.** week   has   days

lundi	**mardi**	**mercredi**	**jeudi**	**vendredi**	**samedi**	**dimanche**
1	2	3	4	5	6	7

(eel) *(tray)* *(za$^{(n)}$-por-tah$^{(n)}$)*
Il est trés important to know the days of the week **et** the various parts of the day. Let's
it is very

learn them. Be sure to say them aloud before filling in the blanks below. **Les** *(frah$^{(n)}$-say)* **Français**
the   French

begin counting their week on Monday with **lundi.**

(lun-dee)
lundi _lundi, lundi_____

(mar-dee)
mardi_____

(mare-kruh-dee)
mercredi_____

(zhuh-dee)
jeudi_____

(vah$^{(n)}$-druh-dee)
vendredi_____

(sahm-dee)
samedi_____

(dee-mah$^{(n)}$-sh)
dimanche_____

(oh-zhoor-dwee) *(duh-ma$^{(n)}$)* *(ee-air)(say-tay)*
If **aujourd'hui c'est mercredi,** then **demain c'est jeudi et hier c'était mardi.**
was

Maintenant, you supply **les réponses correctes.** If **aujourd'hui c'est lundi,** then

demain c'est _____ **et hier c'était**_____. **Ou,** if **aujourd'hui est lundi,**

then _____ **c'est mardi et** _____ _hier_ _____ **c'était dimanche.** *(kel)* *(zhoor)* **Quel jour**
what   day

(ess) *(say)*
est-ce aujourd'hui? Aujourd'hui c'est _____.
is   it

(ma$^{(n)}$-tuh-nah$^{(n)}$)
Maintenant, peel off the next **sept** labels **et** put them on a *(kah-lah$^{(n)}$-dree-ay)* **calendrier** you use every day.

From **aujourd'hui** on, Monday **c'est "lundi."**

☐ **le filtre** *(feel-truh)* . . . . filter   _____

  — **un café filtre** *(kah-fay feel-truh)* . . . . . . filtered coffee   _____

☐ **la fin** *(fa$^{(n)}$)* . . . . end   _____

☐ **le fonctionnaire** *(foh$^{(n)}$-see-oh-nair)* . . . . . functionary, civil servant   _____

☐ **le football** *(foot-bahl)* . . . . soccer   _____

There are **quatre** parts to each **jour.**
day

morning = **matin** *(ma-ta[n])*

afternoon = **après-midi** *(ah-pray-mee-dee)*   *après-midi, après-midi*

evening = **soir** *(swahr)*

night = **nuit** *(nwee)*

Notice that the French days of the week are not capitalized as **en anglais.** **Maintenant,** *(ma[n]-tuh-nah[n])*

fill in the following blanks **et** then check your **réponses** at the bottom of **la page.**

a.	Sunday morning	= *dimanche matin, dimanche matin*
b.	Friday evening	=
c.	Saturday evening	=
d.	Monday morning	=
e.	Wednesday morning	=
f.	Tuesday afternoon	=
g.	Thursday afternoon	=
h.	Thursday night	=
i.	yesterday evening	=
j.	yesterday morning	=
k.	tomorrow evening	=
l.	tomorrow afternoon	=
m.	yesterday afternoon	=

RÉPONSES

a.	dimanche matin	e.	mercredi matin	i.	hier soir
b.	vendredi soir	f.	mardi après-midi	j.	hier matin
c.	samedi soir	g.	jeudi après-midi	k.	demain soir
d.	lundi matin	h.	jeudi nuit	l.	demain après-midi
				m.	hier après-midi

21

So, **avec** merely **onze mots** you can specify any day of the (suh-men) **semaine** et any time of the (zhoor) **jour.**
week

Les mots "(oh-zhoor-dwee) <u>**aujord'hui**</u>," "(duh-ma$^{(n)}$) <u>**demain**</u>" et "(ee-air) <u>**hier**</u>" will be (tray) **très** (za$^{(n)}$-por-tah$^{(n)}$) **importants** for you in making

(ray-zair-vah-see-oh$^{(n)}$) **réservations** et (rah$^{(n)}$-day-voo) **rendez-vous,** in getting (bee-yay) **billets** (duh) **de** (tay-ah-truh) **théâtre** et many things you will wish
reservations   appointments   theater tickets

to do.   Knowing the parts of **le jour** will help you to learn **et** understand the various

(sah-lew-tah-see-oh$^{(n)}$) (frah$^{(n)}$-sez) **salutations   françaises** below. Practice these every day now until your trip.
greetings

good morning good afternoon	=	(boh$^{(n)}$-zhoor) **bonjour**
good evening	=	(boh$^{(n)}$-swahr) **bonsoir**
good night	=	(bun) (nwee) **bonne nuit**
hi!	=	(sah-lew) **salut**

salut, salut, salut

Take the next **quatre** labels **et** stick them on the appropriate (showz) **choses** in your (maze-oh$^{(n)}$) **maison.** How
things

about the bathroom mirror **pour** (poor) "**bonjour**"? **Ou** the front door **pour** "**bonsoir**"? **Ou**
for

your alarm clock **pour** "**bonne nuit**"? Remember that whenever you enter small shops **et**

stores **en France** you will hear the appropriate (sah-lew-tah-see-oh$^{(n)}$) **salutation** for the time of day. Don't be

surprised. It is a (tray) **très** friendly **et** warm (koo-tewm) **coutume.** Everyone greets everyone **et** you
custom

should too, if you really want to enjoy **la France.** You (et) **êtes** about one-fourth of your way
are

through **le** (lee-vruh) **livre** et (say) **c'est** a good time to quickly review **les mots** you have learned before
it is

doing the crossword puzzle on the next **page.** (ah-mew-zay-voo) **Amusez-vous** et (bun) **bonne** (shah$^{(n)}$s) **chance.** **Ou** as we
amuse yourself   good   luck

say **en anglais,** have fun and good luck.

RÉPONSES TO CROSSWORD PUZZLE (MOTS CROISÉS)

ACROSS		DOWN	
1. je voudrais	16. cinquante	1. jour	16. pourquoi
2. avec	17. pendule	2. carte postale	17. pièce
3. avoir	18. aujord'hui	3. noir	18. lampe
4. Amérique	19. lumière	4. l'après-midi	19. mur
5. monnaie	20. eau	5. plafond	20. rouge
6. ticket d'autobus	21. cinq	6. réponse	21. vert
7. samedi	22. quatre	7. salut	22. vendredi
8. banque	23. et	8. qui	23. maison
9. dix-neuf	24. voilà	9. qu'est-ce que c'est	24. coin
10. nuit	25. comment	10. argent	25. gris
11. thé	26. jaune	11. femme	26. combien
12. vingt	27. multicolore	12. un	27. quand
13. mercredi	28. trois	13. mardi	28. deux
14. chaise	29. tableau	14. nous avons	
15. homme	30. rideau	15. blanc	

CROSSWORD PUZZLE (MOTS CROISÉS) *(kwah-zay)*

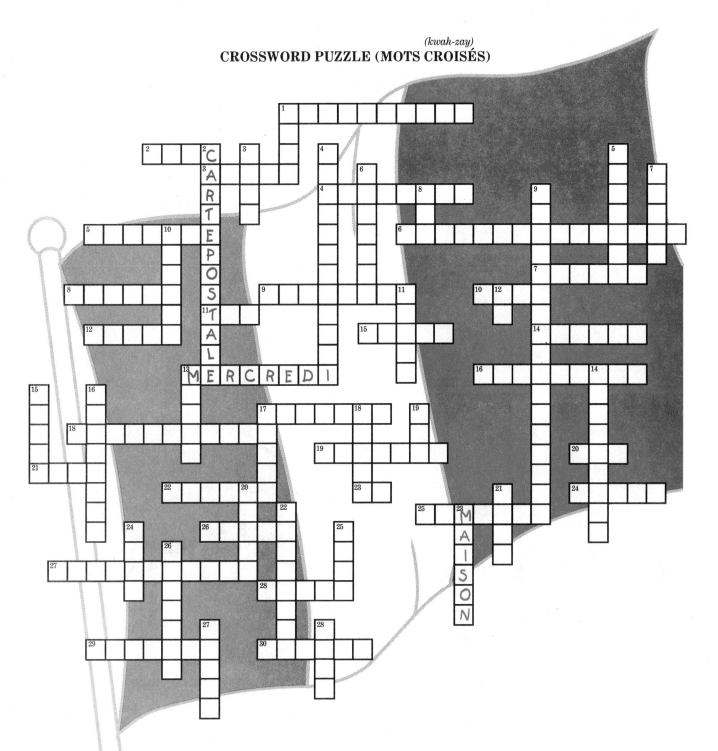

<table>
<tr><td colspan="2">

ACROSS

</td><td colspan="2">

DOWN

</td></tr>
<tr><td>

1. I would like
2. with
3. to have
4. America
5. coins
6. bus ticket
7. Saturday
8. bank
9. 19
10. night
11. tea
12. 20
13. Wednesday
14. chair
15. man

</td><td>

16. 50
17. clock
18. today
19. light
20. water
21. five
22. four
23. and
24. there is
25. how?
26. yellow
27. multi-colored
28. three
29. picture
30. curtain

</td><td>

1. day
2. postcard
3. black
4. the afternoon
5. ceiling
6. response, answer
7. hi
8. who?
9. what is it?
10. money
11. woman
12. a (masculine)
13. Tuesday
14. we have
15. white

</td><td>

16. why?
17. room
18. lamp
19. wall
20. red
21. green
22. Friday
23. house
24. corner
25. gray
26. how much?
27. when?
28. two

</td></tr>
</table>

23

Step 8

(dah⁽ⁿ⁾) *(sewr)* *(soo)*
Dans, sur, sous . . .
in   on   under

(pray-poh-zee-see-oh⁽ⁿ⁾) *(frah⁽ⁿ⁾-sez)*
Les prépositions françaises (words like "in," "on," "through," and "next to") **sont** easy
are

to learn **et** they allow you to be precise **avec** a minimum of effort. Instead of having to

(sees)
point **six** times at a piece of yummy pastry you wish to order, you can explain precisely

(eel)
which one you want by saying **il est** behind, in front of, next to, **ou** under the piece of
it   is

(puh-tee)
pastry which the salesperson is starting to pick up. Let's learn some of these **petits mots**
little

(tray) *(see-mee-lair)* *(eg-zah⁽ⁿ⁾-pluh)*
which **sont très similaires** to **anglais**. Study the **exemples** below.

(duh)   *(soo)*
de* = out of/from   *(ah koh-tay duh)*   **sous** = under
(dah⁽ⁿ⁾)   **à côté de*** = next to   *(oh-duh-sue duh)*
dans = into/in   **au-dessus de*** = over

(ah⁽ⁿ⁾-truh) *(noo-vel)* *(oh-tell)*
L'homme entre <u>dans</u> le nouvel hôtel.
goes   new

(noo-voh)
Le nouveau tableau est <u>au-dessus de</u> la table.
new

Le nouveau tableau est <u>à côté de</u> l'horloge.
(lor-lozh)
large clock

(vee-a⁽ⁿ⁾) *(lek-say-lah⁽ⁿ⁾)*
La femme vient <u>de</u> l'excellent hôtel.
comes

Le chien gris est <u>sous</u> la table marron.

(dew)
La table marron est <u>au-dessus du</u> chien.

(doke-tur) *(bun)*
Le docteur est <u>dans</u> le bon hôtel.
good

(vairt)
L'horloge verte est <u>au-dessus de</u> la table.

L'horloge verte est <u>à côté du</u> tableau.

(de+le)   *(de+les)*
*Remember that **de** sometimes combines with **la, le,** or **les** to form **du, de la, de l'** and **des.**

☐ **la forme** *(form)* . . . . form, shape   _____
☐ **la forêt** *(foh-ray)* . . . . forest   _____
☐ **le foyer** *(fwah-yay)* . . . . home, hearth   _____
☐ **franc/franche** *(frah⁽ⁿ⁾/frah⁽ⁿ⁾sh)* . . . . frank, honest   _____
☐ **le fruit** *(fwee)* . . . . fruit   _____

24

Fill in the blanks below **avec les prépositions correctes** *(pray-poh-zee-see-oh⁽ⁿ⁾)* according to the **images** on the
previous **page**.
_{pictures} *(ee-mahzh)*

L'homme entre *(ah⁽ⁿ⁾-truh)* _____ le nouvel hôtel.   Le chien gris est _____ la table.

L'horloge verte est *(lor-lozh)* *(vairt)* _____ la table.   Le docteur est _dans_ le bon hôtel.

L'horloge verte est _____ du tableau.   Le nouveau tableau est *(noo-voh)* _____ la table.

La table marron est _____ le tableau.   Le nouveau tableau est _____ l'horloge.

La femme vient *(fahm)* _____ l'excellent hôtel.   La table marron est _____ l'horloge.

Maintenant, répondez aux questions *(ma⁽ⁿ⁾-tuh-nah⁽ⁿ⁾)* *(oh)* *(kehs-tee-oh⁽ⁿ⁾)* based on **les images** *(lay)* *(zee-mahzh)* on the previous **page**.
_{to the}

Où est le docteur? _____

Où est le chien? *(shee-ya⁽ⁿ⁾)* _____

Où est la table? _____

Où est le tableau? _____

Que fait la femme? *(kuh)* *(fay)* _____
_{does}

Que fait l'homme? *(fay)* _____
_{does}

L'horloge est-elle verte? _Oui, l'horloge est verte._
_{is   it}

Le chien est-il gris? _Oui,_
_{is   it}

☐ **la glace** *(glahs)* . . . . ice, ice cream   _____
☐ **la galerie** *(gah-lur-ee)* . . . . gallery, long room   _____
☐ **la géographie** *(zhay-oo-grah-fee)* . . . . geography   _____
☐ **la gomme** *(gohm)* . . . . eraser   _____
☐ **le gourmand** *(gour-mah⁽ⁿ⁾)* . . . . gourmand, glutton   _____

Maintenant for some more practice **avec les prépositions françaises.**

> *(sewr)*
> **sur** = on
>
> *(ah⁽ⁿ⁾-truh)*
> **entre** = between
>
> *(duh-vah⁽ⁿ⁾)*
> **devant** = in front of
>
> *(dare-ee-air)*
> **derrière** = behind

(vair) *(doe)* *(sewr)*
Le verre d'eau est sur la table.

Le verre d'eau est _____ **la table.**

Le tableau multicolore est sur le mur.

Le tableau multicolore est _____*sur*_____ **le mur.**

(dare-ee-air)
La lampe jaune est derrière la table.

La lampe jaune est _____ **la table.**

(duh-vah⁽ⁿ⁾) *(lee)*
La table marron est devant le lit.
bed

La table est _____ **le lit.**

(ah⁽ⁿ⁾-truh)
**La lampe jaune est entre la table et
le lit.**

La lampe jaune est _____ **la table et
le lit.**

(oh)
Répondez aux questions, based on **les images,** by filling in the blanks **avec les**
to the

prépositions correctes. Choose **les prépositions** from those you have just learned.

Où est le livre rouge?

Le livre rouge est _____ **la table marron.**

Où est l'autobus bleu?

L'autobus bleu est _____ **l'hôtel gris.**

- ☐ **le gourmet** *(gour-may)* . . . . gourmet, epicure   _____
- ☐ **le gouvernement** *(goo-vair-nuh-mah⁽ⁿ⁾)* . . . . . government   _____
- ☐ **grand** *(grah⁽ⁿ⁾)* . . . . big   _____
- ☐ **la grandeur** *(grah⁽ⁿ⁾-dur)* . . . . greatness   _____

26 ☐ **le guide** *(geed)* . . . . guide   _____

Où est le téléphone gris? *(tay-lay-phone)* *(gree)* **Où est le tapis vert?** *(tah-pee)* *(vair)* **Où est le tableau?**

Le téléphone est_____ le mur blanc.

Le téléphone est_____ du tableau multicolore.

Le téléphone est *au-dessus de*___ la table noire.

Le tapis vert est_____ la table noire.

Le tableau est_____ le mur blanc.

Maintenant, fill in each blank on **le château** below **avec** the best possible **préposition.**
(shah-toe)
castle

Les réponses correctes sont at the bottom of **la page.   Amusez-vous.**
have fun

1. _____

2. _____

5. _____

3. _____

9. _____

8. _____

4. _____

6. _____

7. *à côté de*

10. _____

RÉPONSES				
1. au-dessus de	3. derrière	5. dans	7. à côté de	9. sous
2. sur	4. entre	6. dans	8. devant	10. de

27

Step 9

(oh⁽ⁿ⁾) *(sep-tah⁽ⁿ⁾m-bruh)* *(ah-vreel)* *(zhoo-a⁽ⁿ⁾)* *(no-vah⁽ⁿ⁾m-bruh)*
Trente jours ont septembre, avril, juin et novembre . . .
⠀⠀⠀⠀⠀⠀⠀⠀⠀⠀⠀⠀have

(suh-men)
Sound familiar? You have learned the days of **la semaine,** so **maintenant c'est le**
⠀⠀⠀it is

(mow-mah⁽ⁿ⁾) ⠀⠀⠀⠀⠀⠀⠀*(mwah)* *(duh)* *(lah-nay)* ⠀⠀⠀⠀⠀⠀⠀⠀⠀*(tah⁽ⁿ⁾)*
moment to learn **les mois de** **l'année et** all kinds of **temps** which you might encounter on
⠀⠀⠀⠀⠀⠀⠀⠀⠀⠀⠀⠀⠀months⠀of⠀the year⠀⠀⠀⠀⠀⠀⠀⠀⠀⠀⠀⠀weather

⠀⠀⠀⠀⠀⠀⠀⠀⠀⠀⠀⠀⠀*(eg-zah⁽ⁿ⁾-pluh)* ⠀⠀⠀⠀⠀⠀⠀⠀⠀⠀⠀⠀*(tah⁽ⁿ⁾)*
your holiday. For **exemple,** you ask about **le temps en français** just as you would **en**

⠀⠀⠀⠀⠀⠀*(kel)* ⠀⠀⠀⠀⠀⠀*(fay-teel)*
anglais— **"Quel temps fait-il aujourd'hui?"** Practice all the possible answers to this
⠀⠀⠀⠀⠀⠀what⠀⠀weather⠀⠀does it do⠀⠀today

(kehs-tee-oh⁽ⁿ⁾) *(pwee)*
question et puis write **les réponses** in the blanks below.
⠀⠀⠀⠀⠀⠀⠀⠀⠀then

(kel) ⠀⠀*(tah⁽ⁿ⁾)* ⠀⠀*(fay-teel)* *(oh-zhoor-dwee)*
Quel temps fait-il aujourd'hui?

(eel) (pluh)
Il pleut aujourd'hui. _____
⠀⠀rains

(nehzh)
Il neige aujourd'hui. _____ *Il neige aujourd'hui.* _____
⠀snows

(fay) (fray)
Il fait frais aujourd'hui. _____
⠀⠀⠀cool

(fwah)
Il fait froid aujourd'hui. _____
⠀⠀⠀cold

(boh)
Il fait beau aujourd'hui. _____
⠀⠀⠀nice

(mow-vay)
Il fait mauvais aujourd'hui. _____
⠀⠀⠀bad

(show)
Il fait chaud aujourd'hui. _____
⠀⠀⠀hot

(dew) (broo-ee-yar)
Il fait du brouillard aujourd'hui. _____
⠀⠀⠀⠀foggy

(ma⁽ⁿ⁾-tuh-nah⁽ⁿ⁾) ⠀⠀⠀⠀⠀⠀⠀⠀⠀⠀⠀⠀⠀⠀⠀⠀⠀⠀⠀⠀⠀⠀⠀⠀⠀⠀⠀*(pwee)*
Maintenant, practice **les mots** on the next **page** aloud **et puis** fill in the blanks with **les**
⠀⠀then

(noh⁽ⁿ⁾) ⠀⠀⠀*(mwah)*
noms of **les mois et** the appropriate weather report. Notice that **en français,** the months
names⠀⠀⠀⠀months

of the year and the days of the week are not capitalized.

☐ **l'identification** *(lee-dah⁽ⁿ⁾-tee-fee-kah-see-oh⁽ⁿ⁾)* . . . . identification⠀⠀_____
☐ **l'île** *(leel)* . . . . island⠀⠀⠀⠀⠀_____
☐ **l'importance** *(la⁽ⁿ⁾-por-tah⁽ⁿ⁾s)* . . . . importance⠀⠀_____
⠀⠀— **une chose importante** *(a⁽ⁿ⁾-por-tah⁽ⁿ⁾t)* . . . . . . an important thing⠀_____
28 ☐ **inacceptable** *(een-ahk-sep-tahb-luh)* . . . . unacceptable⠀⠀_____

(ah⁽ⁿ⁾*) (zhah*⁽ⁿ⁾*-vee-ay)*
en janvier _____

(nehzh)
Il neige en janvier. _____

(fay-vree-ay)
en février _____

(oh-see)
Il neige aussi en février. _____
also

(mars)
en mars _____*en mars*_____

(pluh)
Il pleut en mars. _____

(ah-vreel)
en avril _____

Il pleut aussi en avril. _____

(may)
en mai _____

(fay) (dew) (vah⁽ⁿ⁾*)*
Il fait du vent en mai. _____
windy

(zhoo-a⁽ⁿ⁾*)*
en juin _____

(fay) (so-lay)
Il fait du soleil en juin. _____
sunny

(zhwee-ay)
en juillet _____

(boh)
Il fait beau en juillet. ___*Il fait beau en juillet.*___

(oot)
en août _____

(show)
Il fait chaud en août. _____

(sep-tah⁽ⁿ⁾*m-bruh)*
en septembre _____

(broo-ee-yar)
Il fait du brouillard en septembre. _____
foggy

(ok-toh-bruh)
en octobre _____

(fray)
Il fait frais en octobre. _____

(no-vah⁽ⁿ⁾*m-bruh)*
en novembre _____

(mow-vay)
Il fait mauvais en novembre. _____

(day-sah⁽ⁿ⁾*m-bruh)*
en décembre _____

Il fait froid en décembre. _____

Maintenant, répondez aux questions based on **les images** to the right.

Quel temps fait-il en février? *Il fait* _____
in

Quel temps fait-il en avril? _____

Quel temps fait-il en mai? _____

Quel temps fait-il en août? _____

Quel temps fait-il aujourd'hui, beau ou mauvais? _____

☐ impossible *(a*⁽ⁿ⁾*-poh-see-bluh)* . . . . impossible _____
— C'est impossible! *(say ta*⁽ⁿ⁾*-poh-see-bluh)* . . It's impossible! _____
☐ l'industrie *(la*⁽ⁿ⁾*-dew-stree)* . . . . industry _____
☐ l'information *(la*⁽ⁿ⁾*-for-mah-see-oh*⁽ⁿ⁾*)* . .nehzh information _____
☐ l'ingénieur *(la*⁽ⁿ⁾*-zhay-nee-ur)* . . . . engineer _____

Maintenant, les saisons de l'année . . .
(say-zoh(n))
seasons

| *(lee-vair)* **l'hiver** winter | *(lay-tay)* **l'été** summer | *(loh-tone)* **l'automne** autumn | *(prah(n)-tah(n))* **le printemps** spring |

l'été

| **Il fait froid** *(ah(n)) (nee-vair)* **en hiver.** | **Il fait chaud** *(ah(n)) (nay-tay)* **en été.** | **Il fait du vent** *(ah(n)) (noh-tone)* **en automne.** | **Il pleut** *(oh)* **au printemps.** |

At this point, **c'est une bonne idée** to familiarize yourself **avec les températures**
(say) (tewn) (bun) (ee-day) — it is a good idea — *(tah(n)-pay-rah-tewr)* temperatures

(uh-roh-pay-yen)
européennes. Carefully read the typical weather forecasts below **et** study **le**
European

(tair-moh-meh-truh) *(uh-rope)*
thermomètre because **les températures en Europe** are calculated on the basis of
thermometer

Centigrade (not Fahrenheit).

Fahrenheit | Celsius

Fahrenheit	Celsius	
212° F	100° C	*(low) (boo)* **l'eau bout** boils
98.6° F	37° C	**la température normale du sang** of blood
68° F	20° C	
32° F	0° C	**l'eau douce gèle** water fresh freezes
0° F	-17.8° C	**l'eau salée gèle** water salt freezes
-10° F	-23.3° C	

Le temps pour lundi, le 21 mars:

> froid avec du vent
> *(duh-gray)*
> température: 5 degrés
> degrees

Le temps pour mardi, le 18 juillet:

> beau et chaud
> température: 20 degrés

☐ **l'inscription** *(la(n)-screep-see-oh(n))* . . . . inscription _____
☐ **l'institut** *(la(n)-stee-tew)* . . . . institute _____
☐ **intéressant** *(a(n)-tay-ray-sah(n))* . . . . interesting _____
☐ **l'Italie** *(lee-tah-lee)* . . . . Italy _____
— **italien** *(ee-tah-lee-a(n))* . . . . Italian _____

Foyer, faim et foi
(fwah-yay) *(fa⁽ⁿ⁾)* *(fwah)*
home   hunger   faith

Just as we have the 3 "R's" **en anglais, en français** there are the 3 "F's" which help us to understand some of the basics of **la vie française.**
(vee) *(frah⁽ⁿ⁾-sez)*
life   French

Foyer

Faim

Foi

Study **les images** below **et puis** write out **les nouveaux mots** in the blanks which follow.
(pwee)   *(noo-voh)*
new

L'Arbre généalogique
(lahr-bruh) *(zhay-nay-ah-loh-zheek)*
tree   genealogical

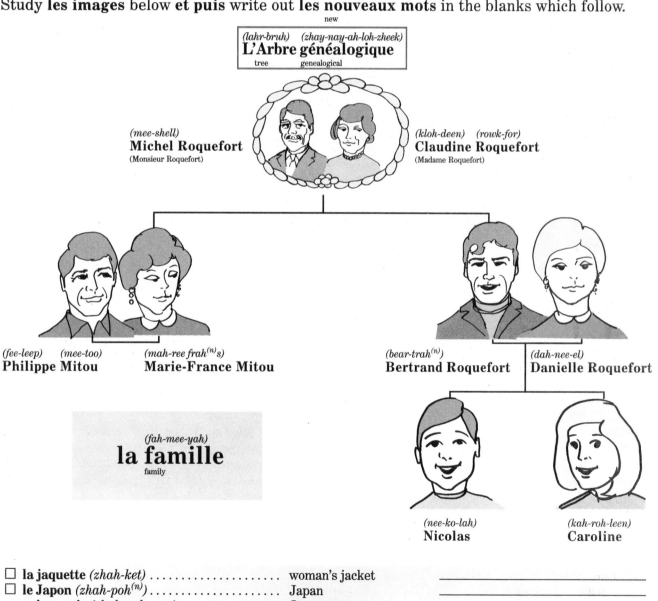

(mee-shell)
Michel Roquefort
(Monsieur Roquefort)

(kloh-deen) *(rowk-for)*
Claudine Roquefort
(Madame Roquefort)

(fee-leep) *(mee-too)*
Philippe Mitou

(mah-ree frah⁽ⁿ⁾s)
Marie-France Mitou

(bear-trah⁽ⁿ⁾)
Bertrand Roquefort

(dah-nee-el)
Danielle Roquefort

(fah-mee-yah)
la famille
family

(nee-ko-lah)
Nicolas

(kah-roh-leen)
Caroline

☐ **la jaquette** *(zhah-ket)* . . . . woman's jacket   _____
☐ **le Japon** *(zhah-poh⁽ⁿ⁾)* . . . . Japan   _____
  — japonais *(zhah-poh-nay)* . . . . Japanese   _____
☐ **le journal** *(zhoor-nahl)* . . . . newspaper   _____
☐ **La Joconde** *(zhoh-kohnd)* . . . . Mona Lisa in the Louvre   _____

(grah⁽ⁿ⁾-pah-rah⁽ⁿ⁾)
les grands-parents
grandparents

(pah-rah⁽ⁿ⁾)
les parents
parents

(grah⁽ⁿ⁾-pear)
le grand-père _le grand-père_
grandfather

(pear)
le père _____
father

(grah⁽ⁿ⁾-mare)
la grand-mère _____
grandmother

(mare)
la mère _____
mother

(lay) (zah⁽ⁿ⁾-fah⁽ⁿ⁾)
les enfants
children

(pah-rah⁽ⁿ⁾)
les parents
relatives

(fees)
le fils _____
son

(loh⁽ⁿ⁾-kluh)
l'oncle _____
uncle

(fee-yah)
la fille _____
daughter

(taunt)
la tante _____
aunt

(frair) *(suhr)*
Le fils et la fille sont aussi frère et soeur.
brother   sister

Let's learn how to identify **la** *(fah-mee-yah)* **famille** by *(noh⁽ⁿ⁾)* **nom.** Study the following **exemples.**
family   name

(sah-pell)
Comment s'appelle le père?
how   is called   the father

Le père s'appelle _Bertrand_ .
is called

Comment s'appelle la mère?
is called

La mère s'appelle _Danielle_ .
is called

Maintenant, you fill in the following blanks, *(bah-zay) (sewr)* **basés sur les images,** in the same manner.
based   on

(sah-pell)
Comment s'appelle _le fils_ ?

_____ **s'appelle** _____ .

Comment s'appelle _____ ?

_____ **s'appelle** _____ .

☐ **juste** *(zhoost)* . . . . fair, just _____
☐ **la justice** *(zhoo-stees)* . . . . justice _____
☐ **le kilomètre** *(kee-loh-meh-truh)* . . . . kilometer (=.624 miles) _____
☐ **le kiosque** *(kee-ohsk)* . . . . kiosk _____
32 ☐ **le kilo** *(kee-loh)* . . . . kilo (=2.2 pounds) _____

Study all these **images et puis** practice

saying **et** writing out **les mots.**

Voilà la cuisine.
(lah)

(ray-free-zhay-rah-tuhr)
le réfrigérateur

_____

(kwee-zee-nee-air)
la cuisinière
stove

_____

(va^{(n)})
le vin

_____

(bee-air)
la bière

_____

(lay)
le lait

le lait

(buhr)
le beurre

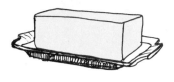

_____

Répondez aux questions aloud.

Où est la bière? . . . . **La bière est la dans le réfrigérateur.**
(ray-free-zhay-rah-tuhr)

Où est le lait?   **Où est le vin?**   **Où est le beurre?**
(luh)

☐ **le lac** *(lack)* . . . . lake   _____
☐ **le langage** *(lah^{(n)}-gahzh)* . . . . language   _____
☐ **la leçon** *(lay-soh^{(n)})* . . . . lesson   _____
☐ **la lecture** *(lek-tewr)* . . . . reading   _____
☐ **la liberté** *(lee-bear-tay)* . . . . liberty   _____

33

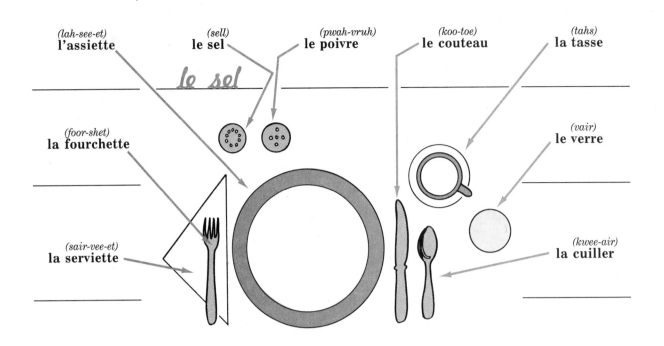

(lah-see-et)
l'assiette

(sell)
le sel

(pwah-vruh)
le poivre

(koo-toe)
le couteau

(tahs)
la tasse

le sel

(foor-shet)
la fourchette

(vair)
le verre

(sair-vee-et)
la serviette

(kwee-air)
la cuiller

(plah-kar)
le placard

(pa$^{(n)}$)
le pain

(tay)
le thé

(kah-fay)
le café

le thé

Où est le pain? Le pain est dans le placard. Où est le thé? Où est le café? Où est

le sel? Où est le poivre? Maintenant ^(*(oo-vray)*)**ouvrez** your **livre** to the **page avec** the labels **et**
_{open}

remove the next group of labels **et** proceed to label all these **choses** in your **maison.** Do

not forget to use every opportunity to say these **mots** out loud. ^(*(say)*)**C'est très** ^(*(a$^{(n)}$-por-tah$^{(n)}$)*)**important!**

☐ **le lieu** *(lee-uh)* . . . . place _____
☐ **la ligne** *(leen-yuh)* . . . . line _____
☐ **la limonade** *(lee-mow-nod)* . . . . lemonade _____
☐ **le logement** *(lohz-mah$^{(n)}$)* . . . . lodging _____
☐ **Londres** *(loh$^{(n)}$-druh)* . . . . London _____

En France, there is not the wide variety of **religions** that **nous avons ici en Amérique.**
(ruh-lee-zhee-oh[n]) *(new)* *(zah-voh[n])*
religions   we   have

A person's **religion est généralement** one of the following:
(ruh-lee-zhee-oh[n]) *(zhay-nay-rahl-mah[n])*
generally

1. **catholique** _____ *catholique* _____
   (kah-toe-leek)
   Catholic

2. **protestant** _____
   (pro-teh-stah[n])
   Protestant

3. **juif** _____
   (zhew-eef)
   Jewish

4. **musulman** _____
   (mew-zewl-mah[n])
   Moslem

Voilà une cathédrale en France.
(kah-tay-drahl)
cathedral

Est-ce une cathédrale catholique

ou protestante? Est-ce une nouvelle
(pro-teh-stah[n]t)*

cathédrale? Non, c'est une vieille
(say) *(vee-ay)*
old

cathédrale. You will see **beaucoup**
(boh-koo)
many

de belles cathédrales like this during
(bell)
beautiful

your holiday **en France.**

Maintenant let's learn how to say "I am" **en français:** I am = **je suis** _____
(zhuh) *(swee)*

Practice saying **"je suis" avec** the following **mots. Maintenant** write each sentence for

more practice.

Je suis catholique. _____ **Je suis protestant.** _____

Je suis juif. _____ *Je suis juif.* _____ **Je suis américain.** _____

Je suis en Europe. _____ **Je suis en France.** _____
(uh-rope)

*To make an adjective feminine **en français,** all you need to do is add an "e." This will sometimes vary the
pronunciation slightly.

☐ **le magasin** *(ma-gah-za[n])* .... store _____
☐ **le magazine** *(ma-gah-zeen)* .... magazine _____
☐ **magnifique** *(mahn-ee-feek)* .... magnificent _____
☐ **le marchand** *(mar-shah[n])* .... merchant _____
☐ **le mécanicien** *(may-kah-nee-see-a[n])* ...... mechanic _____

Je suis dans l'église. _(dah⁽ⁿ⁾)_ _____   Je suis dans la cuisine. _____

Je suis la mère. _Je suis la mère._   Je suis le père. _____

Je suis dans l'hôtel. _____   Je suis dans le restaurant. _____

Je suis fatigué. _(fah-tee-gay)_ _____   Je suis à côté de l'église. _____

Maintenant identify all **les personnes** _(pear-sohn)_ (people) **dans le tableau** below.   On the **lignes,** _(leen-yuh)_ (lines) write **le**

mot correct en français for the **personne** corresponding to **le nombre à côté de l'image.**

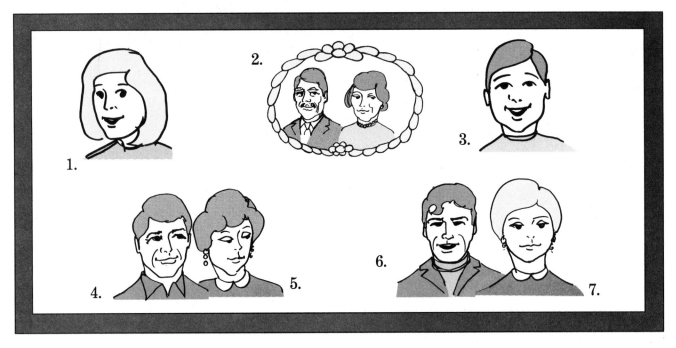

1. _____   2. _____

3. _____   4. _____

5. _la tante, la tante_   6. _____

7. _____

Don't be afraid of all the extra hyphens, apostrophes, accents and uncommon squiggles in

French.   Concentrate on your easy pronunciation guide and remember - practice, practice,

practice.

est-ce = _(ess)_	**qu'est-ce que c'est** = _(kess-kuh-say)_	**s'appelle** = _(sah-pel)_
is it	what is that?	is called

☐ **le marché** _(mar-shay)_ . . . .   market   _____
 — **bon marché** _(boh⁽ⁿ⁾ mar-shay)_ . . . .   cheap   _____
☐ **le mariage** _(mar-ee-ahzh)_ . . . .   marriage, wedding   _____
☐ **le médicament** _(may-dee-kah-mah⁽ⁿ⁾)_ . . . . .   medicine   _____
☐ **la mer** _(mare)_ . . . .   sea   _____

(ah-pruh-nay)
Apprenez!
learn

(voo)
Vous have already used the verbs **avoir** and **voudrais, coûter, arriver, entrer, venir,**
you   *(ah-vwahr)* *(voo-dray)* *(koo-tay)* *(ah-ree-vay)* *(ah*[n]*-tray)* *(vuh-neer)*
                                                                                              to cost

(ray-poh[n]*-druh)* *(ray-pay-tay)* *(ay)*   *(swee)*
répondre, répéter, est, sont, and **suis.** Although you might be able to "get by" **avec** these

(vairb)   *(mee-yuh)*
verbes, let's assume you want to do **mieux** than that. First, a quick review.
                                             better

How do you say ┌─────┐ **en français?** _je_ How do you say ┌─────┐ **en français?** _____
              │ "I" │   │ "we" │
              └─────┘   └─────┘

Compare these **deux** charts

very carefully **et apprenez**
(ah-pruh-nay)
learn

these **sept mots** on the right.

I	=	je *(zhuh)*	we	=	nous *(new)*
he/it	=	il *(eel)*	you	=	vous *(voo)*
she/it	=	elle *(el)*	they	=	ils (masculine) *(eel)*
			they	=	elles (feminine) *(el)*

(leen-yuh) *(ah*[n]*-truh)*
Maintenant draw **lignes entre** the matching **mots anglais et mots français** below to see
                              between

if you can keep these **mots** straight in your mind.

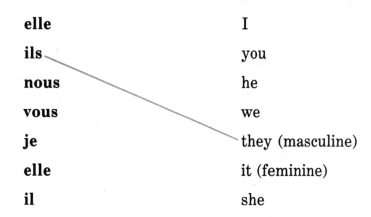

elle	I
ils	you
nous	he
vous	we
je	they (masculine)
elle	it (feminine)
il	she

(ewn) *(fuh-yuh)*
Maintenant close **le livre et** write out both columns of the above practice on **une feuille**

(pah-pee-ay)   *(bee-ya*[n]*)* *(mahl)*   *(pah)*
de papier. How did **vous** do? **Bien ou mal? Pas bien, pas mal? Maintenant** that
                                    well   poorly   not too well   not too badly

(voo)   *(kuh)*   *(day-zee-ray)*
vous know these **mots,** you will soon be able to say almost anything **que vous désirez** by
                                                                          that   desire

using a type of "plug-in" formula.

☐ **le métropolitain** *(may-tro-poh-lee-ta*[n]*)*	subway (metro!)	_____
☐ **la minute** *(mee-newt)*	minute	_____
— **la minuterie** *(mee-new-tuh-ree)*	automatic light switch	_____
☐ **la mode** *(mode)*	fashion	_____
— **à la mode**	fashionable	_____

To demonstrate, here are **six exemples** of very practical **et** important **verbes français.** *(seez)*

These are **verbes** whose basic form ends in **"er."** Write **les verbes** in the blanks below

after **vous** have practiced them out loud many times.

(par-lay)
parler = to speak

(reh-stay)
rester = to remain/stay

(ah-bee-tay)
habiter = to live/reside

_____

rester, rester

_____

(ko-mah⁽ⁿ⁾-day)
commander = to order

(ah-shuh-tay)
acheter = to buy

(saw-puh-lay)
s'appeller = to be called

_____

_____

_____

Study the following verb patterns **avec attention.**

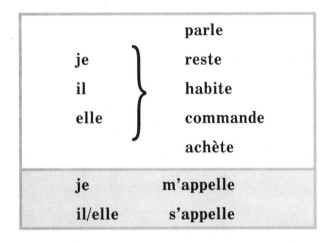

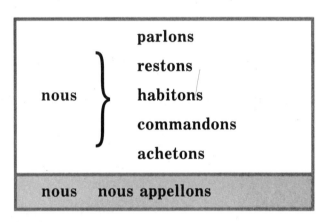

Note: • With **je, il,** or **elle,** you drop the final "r" from the basic verb form.

• With **nous** you drop the final "er" of the basic verb form and substitute "ons" in its place. **Exemple: nous parlons.** *(par-loh⁽ⁿ⁾)*
we speak

• **S'appeler** varies but not too much. It is a very important verb so take a few

extra minutes to learn it.

Some **verbes en français** will not conform to rules quite as easily as these **verbes** do. But

don't worry . . . you will be perfectly understood whether you say **"parle"** or **"parlons."**

Les Français will be delighted that you have taken the time to learn their language.

☐ **le monde** *(mohnd)* . . . . world _____
— **tout le monde** *(too luh mohnd)* . . . . everyone _____
☐ **la montagne** *(moh⁽ⁿ⁾-tahn-yuh)* . . . . mountain _____
☐ **le musée** *(mew-zay)* . . . . museum _____
☐ **la musique** *(mew-zeek)* . . . . music _____

Important! Concentrate on the **similarités** *(see-mee-lar-ee-tay)* of pronunciation **en français** rather than on the spelling. It's really much easier than it looks.

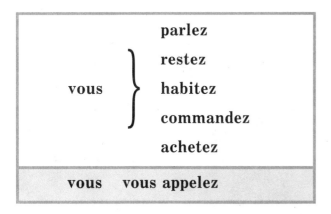
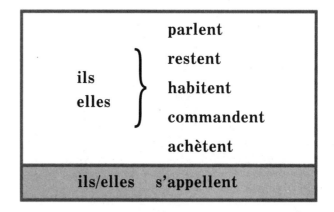

Here are a few hints for mixing and matching verbs and their subjects.

-ons ⟶ nous ex. **nous parlons**   -ent ⟶ ils ex. **ils parlent**
                                               elles ex. **elles parlent**

-ez ⟶ vous ex. **vous parlez**

Maintenant, read through the entire verb form aloud several times before writing out each form in its blank. Notice how despite the difference in spelling, the verbs are pronounced the same (*).

parler

Je* _parle/_____ français.

Il* _parle/_____ français.
Elle

Nous _parlons/_____ français.

Vous _parlez/_____ anglais.

Ils* _parlent/_____ anglais.
Elles

rester

Je* _reste/_____ en France.

Il* _reste/_____ en Amérique.
Elle

Nous _restons/_____ dans un hôtel.

Vous _restez/_____ en Europe.

Ils* _restent/_____ en Belgique.
Elles

☐ **la nation** *(nah-see-oh⁽ⁿ⁾)* . . . . nation   _____
☐ **la nature** *(nah-tewr)* . . . . nature   _____
☐ **naturel** *(nah-tew-rel)* . . . . natural   _____
   — **au naturel** *(oh nah-tew-rel)* . . . . plain, simple   _____
☐ **la nécessité** *(nay-say-see-tay)* . . . . necessity   _____

habiter

J' *habite/* _____ en France.

Il _____ en Amérique.
Elle

Nous _____ en Italie.

Vous _____ en Europe.

Ils _____ en Chine.
Elles

acheter

J' *achète/* _____ un livre.

Il _____ une salade.
Elle

Nous _____ une auto.

Vous _____ une horloge.

Ils _____ une lampe.
Elles

s'appeler

Je _____ Jeanne Guégan.

Il _____ Mitou.
Elle

Nous _____ Smith.

Vous _____ Thierry Huck.

Ils _____ Roquefort.
Elles

commander

Je _____ un verre d'eau.

Il _____ un verre de vin.
Elle

Nous _____ une tasse de thé.

Vous _____ une tasse de café.

Ils _____ un verre de lait.
Elles

Remember these **verbes?**

(vuh-neer)
venir = to come

(ah-lay)
aller = to go

(ah-prah(n)-druh)
apprendre = to learn

_____ *venir, venir* _____   _____   _____

(voo-dray)
voudrais = would like

(ah-vwahr)
avoir = to have

(buh-zwa(n))
avoir besoin de = to need
to have   need   of

_____   _____   _____

Here we have **six,** already familiar **verbes** whose following forms might seem a bit erratic

after our last group.   DON'T PANIC or give up.   Read them out loud, practice them,

think of their **similarités,** write them out and then try to use them in sentences of your own.

☐ **neuf** (*nuf*) . . . . new _____
   — **Le Pont Neuf à Paris** (*poh(n) nuf*) . . . . new bridge in Paris (1604) _____
☐ **Noël** (*no-el*) . . . . Christmas _____
☐ **le nord** (*nor*) . . . . north _____
☐ **Notre-Dame de Paris** (*no-truh dahm*) . . . . Our Lady of Paris

Think of how hard it would be to speak **en anglais** with no verbs — it's the same **en français**.

venir

Je _viens/_ de l'Amérique.

Il _vient/_ de la Belgique.
Elle

Nous _venons/_ du Canada.

Vous _venez/_ de New York.

Ils _viennent/_ de la Suisse.
Elles

aller

Je _vais/_ en France.

Il _va/_ en Italie.
Elle

Nous _allons/_ en Angleterre.

Vous _allez/_ en Europe.

Ils _vont/_ en Chine.
Elles

apprendre

J' _apprends/_ le français.

Il _apprend/_ l'anglais.
Elle

Nous _apprenons/_ la géometrie.

Vous _apprenez/_ l'allemand.

Ils _apprennent/_ l'espagnol.
Elles

voudrais/voudrions

Je _voudrais/_ un verre de vin.

Il _voudrait/_ un verre de vin rouge.
Elle

Nous _voudrions_ un verre de vin blanc.

Vous _voudriez/_ une verre de lait.

Ils _voudraient/_ un verre de bière.
Elles

avoir

J' _ai/_ cinq francs.

Il _a/_ six francs.
Elle

Nous _avons/_ dix francs.

Vous _avez/_ deux francs.

Ils _ont/_ trois francs.
Elles

avoir besoin de

J' _ai besoin_ d'un verre de vin.

Il _____ d'un verre de vin rouge.
Elle

Nous _____ d'un verre de vin blanc.

Vous _____ d'un verre de lait.

Ils _____ d'un verre de bière.
Elles

☐ **l'objet** *(lobe-zhay)* . . . . object _____
☐ **obligatoire** *(oh-blee-gah-twahr)* . . . . compulsory _____
☐ **l'observation** *(lobe-sair-vah-see-oh[n])* . . . . . . observation _____
☐ **l'occupation** *(low-kew-pah-see-oh[n])* . . . . profession, occupation _____
☐ **l'odeur** *(low-dur)* . . . . smell, odor _____

41

Maintenant, take a deep breath.   See if **vous** can fill in the blanks below.   **Les réponses correctes sont** at the bottom of **la page.**

1. I speak French. _____

2. He comes from America. _____

3. We learn French. _____

4. They (masc.) have 10 francs. _____

5. She would like a glass of water. _____

6. We need a room.(chambre) _____ *Nous avons besoin d'une chambre.* ____

7. My name is Paul Smith. _____

8. I live in America. _____

9. You are buying a book. _____

10. He orders a beer. _____

In the following Steps, **vous** will be introduced to more **et** more **verbes et** should drill
them in exactly the same way as **vous** did in this section.   Look up **les nouveaux mots** *(noo-voh)*
in your **dictionnaire et** *(deek-see-oh-nair)* make up your own sentences using the same type of pattern.   Try
dictionary
out your **nouveaux mots** for that's how you make them yours to use on your holiday.

Remember, the more **vous** practice **maintenant,** the more enjoyable your trip will be.

Bonne chance!

Be sure to check off your free **mots** in the box provided as **vous apprenez** each one.

L'Heure
(luhr)
hour

Vous knows how to tell **les jours de la semaine et les mois de l'année**, so maintenant
(lay) days week year

let's learn to tell time. As a **voyageur en France, vous** need to be able to tell time for
(vwhy-ah-zhur) traveler

réservations, rendez-vous et trains. Voilà les "basics."

What time is it? = **Quelle heure est-il?** *(kel) (uhr) (ay-teel)*	half past = **et demie** *(duh-mee)*
_____	less = **moins** *(mwa(n))*
	midnight = **minuit** *minuit* *(mee-nwee)*
	noon = **midi** *(mee-dee)*

Il est cinq heures. Il est quatre heures et demie.

Il est trois heures. Il est deux heures et demie.

Il est midi/minuit.

Il est huit heures vingt.

Il est sept heures quarante. OU Il est huit heures moins vingt.

Maintenant fill in the blanks according to **l'heure** indicated **sur l'horloge.**
(luhr) hour on clock

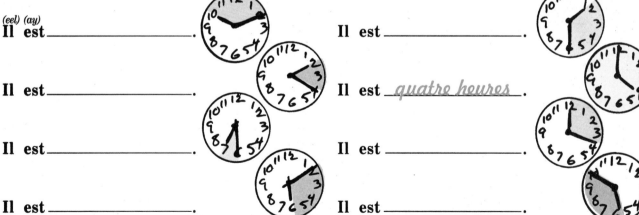

Il est _____ . **Il est** _____ .
(eel) (ay)

Il est _____ . **Il est** *quatre heures* .

Il est _____ . **Il est** _____ .

Il est _____ . **Il est** _____ .

RÉPONSES

(Il est cinq heures cinquante.)
Il est six heures moins dix.   Il est six heures dix.
Il est midi (ou minuit) vingt.
Il est quatre heures.   Il est sept heures et demie.
Il est deux heures vingt.
Il est une heure et demie.   Il est dix heures dix.

Voilà more time-telling **mots** to add to your **mot** power.

un quart *(kahr)*	= a quarter
moins le quart	= a quarter to
et quart	= a quarter past

 Il est deux heures et quart. OU Il est deux heures quinze.

Il est deux heures moins le quart. OU Il est une heure quarante-cinq.

Maintenant, your turn.

 Il est *trois heures et quart*. Il est _____.

Il est _____. Il est _____.

Les nombres — see how **importants** they have become! **Maintenant, répondez aux**

questions **suivantes** *(swee-vah⁽ⁿ⁾t)* based on **les horloges** below.
following

Quelle heure est-il?

1. _____
2. *Il est sept heures et demie.*
3. _____
4. _____
5. _____
6. _____
7. _____

44

When **vous** answer a "**Quand**" question, say "**à**" before you give the time.
_{at}

Quand le train arrive-t-il?_____*à six heures*_____.

TRAIN 43 6:00

(swee-vah⁽ⁿ⁾t)

Maintenant, répondez aux questions suivantes based on **les horloges** below.   Be sure to

practice saying each question out loud several times.

(kah⁽ⁿ⁾) *(koh⁽ⁿ⁾-sair)* *(ko-mah⁽ⁿ⁾s-teel)*
Quand le concert commence-t-il?_____.
_{begins}   _{it}

Quand le film commence-t-il?_____.

Quand l'autobus jaune arrive-t-il?_____.

Quand le taxi arrive-t-il?_____.

(oo-vair)
Quand le restaurant est-il ouvert?____*à cinq heures*____.
_{open}

(fair-may)
Quand le restaurant est-il fermé?_____.
_{closed}

(oh⁽ⁿ⁾)(dee)
À huit heures du matin on dit:
_{in the}   _{one} _{says}
(mah-dahm)
"Bonjour, Madame Dupont."
_{Mrs.}

À huit heures du soir on dit:
_{in the}
(mad-mwah-zel)
"Bonsoir, Mademoiselle Vartan."
_{Miss}

À une heure de l'après-midi on dit:

(muh-see-uh)
"Bonjour, Monsieur Monet."
_{Mr.}

À dix heures du soir on dit:

"Bonne nuit."

☐ **occupé** *(oh-kew-pay)*	busy, occupied	_____
— **une ligne occupée**	engaged telephone line	_____
☐ **officiel** *(oh-fee-see-el)*	official	_____
☐ **l'Orient** *(lor-ee-ah⁽ⁿ⁾)*	Orient	_____
☐ **l'orchestre** *(lor-kess-truh)*	orchestra	_____

Remember:

| What time is it? = | **Quelle heure est-il?** | When/at what time? = | **Quand?** |
| | | | **A quelle heure?** |

Can **vous** pronounce **et** understand **le**

(pah-rah-grahf) *(swee-vah[n])*
paragraphe suivant?
paragraph

> **Le train de Lyon arrive à 15:15. Il est**
>
> **maintenant 15:20. Le train est en** *(ah[n])*
> late
>
> *(ruh-tar)*
> **retard. Le train arrive aujourd'hui**
>
> **à 17:15. Demain le train arrive**
>
> *(ah[n]-kor)*
> **encore à 15:15.**
> again

Voilà more practice exercises. **Répondez aux questions** based on **l'heure** given.

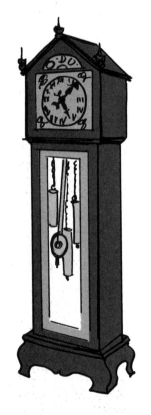

Quelle heure est-il?

1. (10:30) _____

2. (6:30) _____

3. (2:15) *Il est deux heures et quart.*

4. (11:40) _____

5. (12:18) _____

6. (7:20) _____

7. (3:10) _____

8. (4:05) _____

9. (5:35) _____

10. (11:50) _____

46

Voilà a quick quiz.   Fill in the blanks **avec les nombres corrects.**   **Les réponses sont**

(ah⁽ⁿ⁾) (bah)
en   bas.
below

1. **Une minute a**_____**secondes.**
   has   (?)

2. **Une heure a**_____**minutes.**
                        (?)

3. **Un jour a**_____**heures.**
                        (?)

4. **Une semaine a**_____ **jours.**
                          (?)

5. **Un mois a**_____*trente*_____**jours.**
                          (?)

6. **Un an a**_____**mois.**
   year   (?)
   (ah⁽ⁿ⁾)

7. **Un an a**_____**semaines.**
                          (?)

8. **Un an a**_____**jours.**
                          (?)

Voilà a sample page from **un horaire de SNCF** — the French national railroad.   **Un TEE**
                              (or-air)   *(ess-n-say-ef)*
                              timetable

et un rapide (RAP) sont très rapides, un express (EXP) est rapide, et un omnibus (OMN)
                              (rah-peed)
                              fast

(lah⁽ⁿ⁾)
est lent.
slow

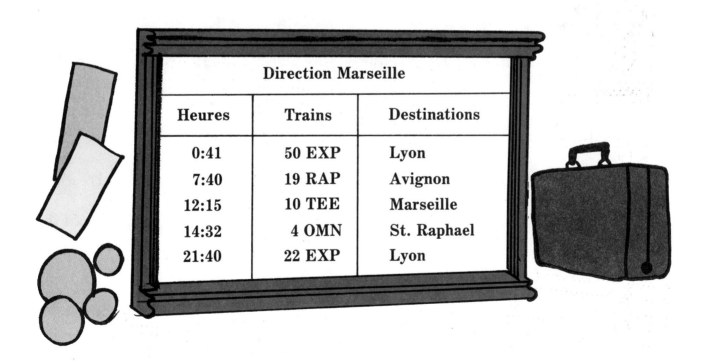

Direction Marseille		
Heures	**Trains**	**Destinations**
0:41	50 EXP	Lyon
7:40	19 RAP	Avignon
12:15	10 TEE	Marseille
14:32	4 OMN	St. Raphael
21:40	22 EXP	Lyon

Voilà trois nouveaux verbes pour *(poor)* Step 12.
for

(deer)
dire = to say

(mah(n)-zhay)
manger = to eat

(bwahr)
boire = to drink

dire, dire _____ _____

dire

Je _dis/_ _____ "Bonjour."

Il _dit/_ _____ "Salut."
Elle

(non(n))
Nous _disons/_ _____ "**Non.**"
no

(wee)
Vous _dites/_ _____ "**Oui.**"
yes

(ree-a(n))
Ils ne _disent/_ _____ **rien.**
Elles *nothing*

manger

Je _mange/_ _____ de la soupe.

Il _____ un bifteck.
Elle

Nous _mangeons/_ _____ beaucoup.

(ree-a(n))
Vous ne _mangez/_ _____ **rien.**
nothing

(ess-kar-go)
Ils _mangent/_ _____ des **escargots.**
Elles *snails*

boire

Je _bois/_ _____ du lait.

Il _boit/_ _____ du vin blanc.
Elle

Nous _buvons/_ _____ des bières.

Vous _buvez/_ _____ une verre d'eau.

Ils _boivent/_ _____ du thé.
Elles

Remember that **"oi"** as in **le verbe "boire"** sounds like "wah." Practice this sound **avec**

(bwah) *(bwah)*
les mots suivants: bois, boit, trois, soixante, mademoiselle, poivre, bonsoir.
pepper

48

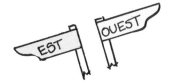

(nor)	*(sood)*	*(est)*	*(west)*
Nord -	**sud,**	**est** -	**ouest**
north	south	east	west

If **vous** are looking at **une carte** *(kart)* **et vous** see **les mots suivants,** it should not be too

difficile *(dee-fee-seal)* to figure out what **ils** *(eel)* mean. Take an educated guess. **Les réponses sont**

en bas. *(ah^(n)) (bah)*

l'Amérique du nord *(lah-may-reek) (dew) (nor)*

la Mer du nord *(mare)*

l'Irelande du nord *(leer-lahnd)*

le Dakota du nord *(dah-koh-tah)*

l'Amérique du sud *(lah-may-reek) (dew) (sood)*

l'Afrique du sud *(lah-freek)*

la Caroline du sud *(kuh-row-leen)*

le Pôle sud *(pole)*

la côte de l'ouest *(koht) (duh) (loo-west)*

la côte de l'est *(koht) (lest)*

les Territoires du nord-ouest *(tay-ree-twahr) (dew) (nor-west)*

le Pôle nord *(pole)*

Les mots français pour north, south, east **et** west **sont** easy to recognize due to their

similarités to **anglais.** So . . .

le nord *(nor)*	=	the north	_____
le sud *(sood)*	=	the south	*le sud*
l'est *(lest)*	=	the east	_____
l'ouest *(loo-west)*	=	the west	_____

du nord *(dew)*	=	northern	_____
du sud	=	southern	_____
de l'est *(duh)*	=	eastern	*de l'est*
de l'ouest	=	western	_____

These **mots sont très importants.** Learn them **aujourd'hui.** But what about more basic

directions *(dee-rek-see-oh^(n))* such as "left," "right," **et** "straight ahead"? Let's learn these **mots.**
directions

gauche *(gohsh)*
left

droite *(dwaht)*
right

straight ahead	=	**tout droit** *(too) (dwah)*
to the left	=	**à gauche** *(ah) (gohsh)*
to the right	=	**à droite** *(ah) (dwaht)*

49

Just as **en anglais**, these **quatre mots** go a long way.

(sill) *(voo)* *(play)* **s'il vous plaît**	=	please _____
(mare-see) **merci**	=	thank you _____ *merci, merci, merci, merci*
(par-doh[n]) **pardon**	=	excuse me _____
(ek-skew-zay-mwah) **excusez-moi**	=	excuse me _____

(koh[n]-vair-sah-see-oh[n]) *(tee-peek)*
Voilà deux conversations typiques pour someone who is trying to find something.
typical

Jean Paul: **Excusez-moi, mais où est l'Hôtel Cézanne?**
(may) but

Claude: **Continuez tout droit, puis tournez à gauche à la deuxième rue et**
(koh[n]-tee-new-ay) *(toor-nay)* *(rew)*
continue   turn   second   street

l'Hôtel est juste à droite.
(zhoost)
just

Jean Paul: **Pardon, Monsieur. Où est le Musée français?**

Claude: **Tournez à droite ici, continuez tout droit approximativement cent**

mètres et puis tournez à gauche et le musée est au coin.
(oh) *(kwa[n])*
on the corner

Are you lost? There is no need to be lost if **vous avez** learned the basic **mots de**
(voo) *(zah-vay)*
have

(dee-rek-see-oh[n])
direction. Do not try to memorize these **conversations** because you will never be looking

for precisely these places. One day you might need to ask for **directions** to **"Maxim's"**

ou "le Louvre" ou "l'Hôtel Maurice." Learn the key **mots de direction et** be sure

(day-stee-nah-see-oh[n])
vous can find your **destination.**
destination

What if the person responding to your **question** answers too quickly for you to understand

the entire reply? If so, ask again, saying,

☐ **la paire** *(pair)*	pair	_____
☐ **le pantalon** *(pah[n]-tah-loh[n])*	pair of trousers	_____
☐ **le Pape** *(pahp)*	Pope	_____
☐ **parfait** *(par-fay)*	perfect	_____
— **C'est parfait**	That's fine.	

Excusez-moi. Je suis américain et je parle seulement un peu de français. Parlez
(suhl-mah^(n)) *(puh)*
only a little
(plew) *(lah^(n)t-mah^(n))* *(voh-truh)* *(boh-koo)*
plus lentement, s'il vous plaît, et répétez votre réponse. Merci beaucoup.
more slowly your

Maintenant **quand** the directions are repeated, **vous** will be able to understand if **vous**
when *(voo)*

(zah-vay)
avez learned the key **mots** for directions. Quiz yourself by filling in the blanks **en bas**
have

avec les mots corrects en français.

Jean-Louis: **Pardon, Mademoiselle. Où est le restaurant "Le Cygne"?**
(seen-yuh)
swan

Chantal: **D'ici, continuez** _____, **puis à la troisième**
(dee-see)
from here   straight ahead   third

_____*rue*_____ **tournez** *à*_____. **Il y a une église. Juste**
street   right   there is

après _____ _____ **encore** _____
the church   turn   *(ah^(n)-kor)*   right
                                                again

et le restaurant "Le Cygne" est _____ , _____*au coin*_____ .
on the left   on the corner

Bonne chance.

Voilà quatre nouveaux verbes.

(ah-tah^(n)-druh)
attendre = to wait for _____*attendre, attendre, attendre,*_____

(koh^(n)-prah^(n)-druh)
comprendre = to understand _____

(vah^(n)-druh)
vendre = to sell _____

(ray-pay-tay)
répéter = to repeat _____

□ **le parc** *(park)* . . . . park   _____
□ **le parfum** *(par-fuh^(n))* . . . . perfume   _____
— **la parfumerie** *(par-few-muh-ree)* . . . . perfumery   _____
□ **le parking** *(par-keeng)* . . . . parking lot   _____
□ **le passeport** *(pass-por)* . . . . passport   _____ 51

As always, say each sentence out loud. Say each and every **mot** carefully, pronouncing each French sound as well as **vous** can.

attendre

J' _attends/_ _____ le train.

Il _attend/_ _____ l'autobus.
Elle

Nous _attendons/_ _____ le taxi.

Vous _____ devant l'hôtel.

Ils _____ Jacques.
Elles

vendre

Je _vends/_ _____ des fleurs.
                        <small>some</small>

Il _vend/_ _____ du fruit.
Elle

Nous _____ une jaquette.

Vous _____ une banane.

Ils _____ <small>(boh-koo)</small> **beaucoup** de tickets.
Elles   <small>a lot</small>

comprendre

Je _comprends/_ _____ l'anglais.

Il _____ le français.
Elle

Nous _comprenons/_ _____ l'italien.

Vous _____ le menu.

Ils _____ le russe.
Elles

répéter

Je _____ le mot.

Il _____ la réponse.
Elle

Nous _____ les noms.

Vous _répétez/_ _____ la leçon.

Ils _____ le verbe.
Elles

Maintenant, see if **vous** can translate the following thoughts **en français**. Les réponses sont en bas.

1. She repeats the word. _____

2. You sell many tickets. _____

3. He waits for the taxi. _Il attend le taxi._

4. We eat some fruit. _____

5. I speak French. _____

6. I drink a cup of tea. _____

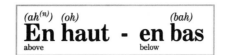

(ah⁽ⁿ⁾) *(oh)* *(bah)*

En haut - en bas

above / below

Step 14

Before **vous commencez** *(koh-mah⁽ⁿ⁾-say)* Step 14, review Step 8. **Maintenant nous apprenons encore** *(ah⁽ⁿ⁾-kor)*

begin

more

des mots.

Voilà une maison en France. *(maze-oh⁽ⁿ⁾)*

La chambre à coucher est en haut. *(shah⁽ⁿ⁾-bruh)* *(koo-shay)*

La salle de bain est aussi en haut. *(sahl)* *(ba⁽ⁿ⁾)*

also

Le bureau est en bas. *(bew-row)*

Le living-room est aussi en bas.

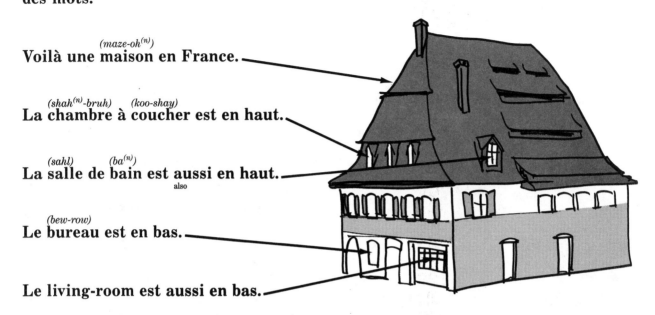

Allez maintenant dans your **chambre à coucher et** look around **la pièce.** *(ah-lay)* *(pea-ess)* Let's

go

learn **les noms des choses dans la chambre** just as **nous avons** *(new)* *(zah-voh⁽ⁿ⁾)* learned the

of the

various parts of **la maison.** Be sure to practice saying **les mots** as you write them

in the spaces **en bas.** Also say out loud the example sentences **sous les images.**

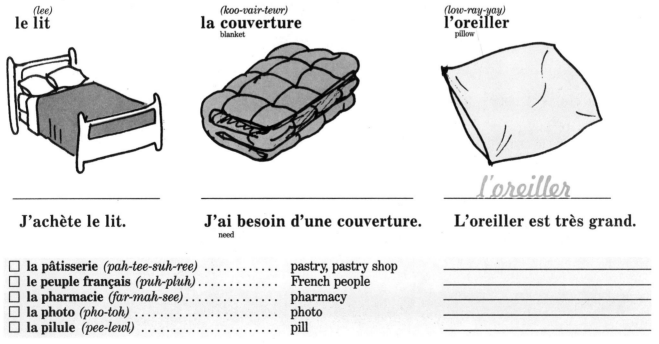

le lit *(lee)*	**la couverture** *(koo-vair-tewr)* blanket	**l'oreiller** *(low-ray-yay)* pillow

l'oreiller

_____ _____ _____

J'achète le lit. **J'ai besoin d'une couverture.** **L'oreiller est très grand.**

need

☐ **la pâtisserie** *(pah-tee-suh-ree)* .... pastry, pastry shop _____

☐ **le peuple français** *(puh-pluh)* .... French people _____

☐ **la pharmacie** *(far-mah-see)* .... pharmacy _____

☐ **la photo** *(pho-toh)* .... photo _____

☐ **la pilule** *(pee-lewl)* .... pill _____ 53

(ray-vay)
le réveil

(lar-mwahr)
l'armoire

Remove the next **cinq** stickers **et** label these **choses dans** your **chambre à coucher.**

_____

J'ai un réveil.

(ee-lee-yah)
Il y a une armoire
there is

dans la chambre.

La chambre dans un hôtel ou une

(oh-bearzh)   *(zhuh-ness)*
auberge de la jeunesse is for sleeping.
youth hostel

dormir = to sleep. This is **un verbe**

(vwhy-ah-zhur)
important pour le voyageur fatigué.
fatigued

Study **les questions et les réponses**

suivantes based on **l'image à gauche.**

---

1. **Où est le réveil?**

   Le réveil est sur la table.

2. **Où est la couverture?**

   La couverture est sur le lit.

3. **Où est l'armoire?**

   L'armoire est dans la chambre.

4. **Où est l'oreiller?**

   L'oreiller est sur le lit.

5. **Où est le lit?**

   Le lit est dans la chambre.

6. **Le lit est-il grand ou petit?**
       is   it big   small
   (puh-tee)

   Le lit n'est pas grand.
        not

   Le lit est petit.

☐ **le pique-nique** *(peek-neek)* . . . . picnic   _____
☐ **la place** *(plahs)* . . . . place, seat   _____
☐ **le plaisir** *(play-zeer)* . . . . pleasure   _____
   — Avec plaisir. . . . . with pleasure   _____
☐ **la police** *(poh-lees)* . . . . police   _____

Maintenant, vous répondez aux questions based on the previous **image.**

Où est le réveil?   **Où est le lit?**

Le réveil est _____   _____

Let's move into **la salle de bain et** do the same thing.

(lah-vah-boh)
le lavabo

(doosh)
la douche

(doo-bul-vay-say)
le W.C.

le lavabo _____

Il y a un lavabo
there is

dans la salle de bain.

_____

La douche n'est pas

dans la chambre d'hôtel.

_____

Le W.C. n'est pas dans la chambre

d'hôtel. Le W.C. et la douche

(kool-wahr)
sont dans le couloir.
hallway

(mir-wahr)
le miroir _____

(glahs)
la glace _____

(sair-vee-et)
les serviettes *les serviettes* _____
towels

(gah⁽ⁿ⁾) *(twah-let)*
le gant de toilette _____
wash glove

(puh-teet) (sair-vee-et)
la petite serviette _____

(ba⁽ⁿ⁾)
la serviette de bain _____

(grahnd)
la grande serviette _____
large   towel

Do not forget to remove **les huit** stickers **suivants et** label these **choses dans** your

salle de bain.

☐ **la politesse** *(poh-lee-tess)* .... politeness   _____
☐ **la politique** *(poh-lee-teek)* .... politics   _____
☐ **le port** *(por)* .... port   _____
☐ **la Préfecture de Police** *(pray-fek-tewr)* ...... Police Headquarters   _____
☐ **premier** *(pruh-mee-ay)* .... first   _____

55

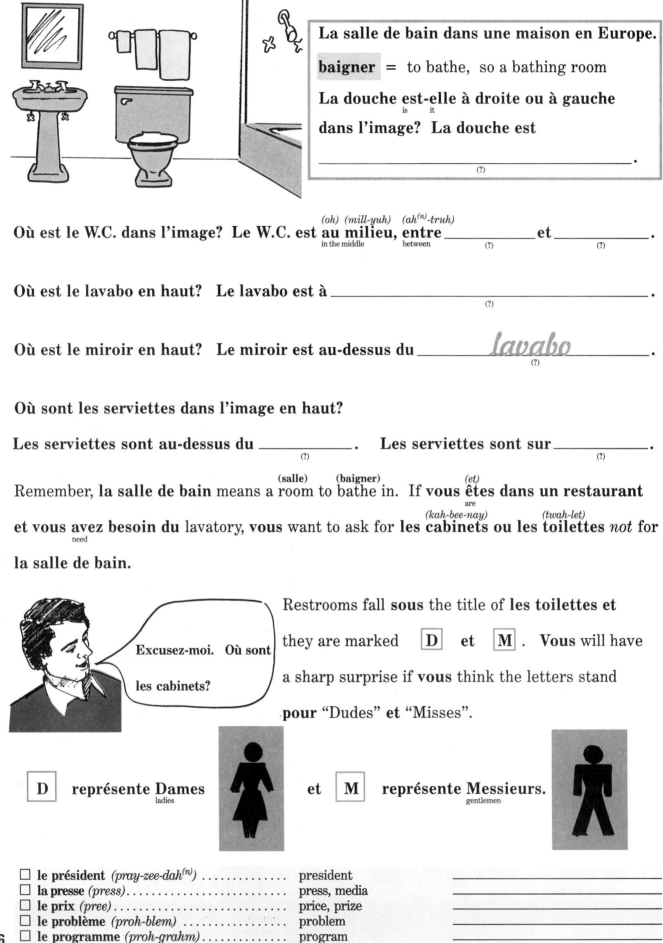

La salle de bain dans une maison en Europe.

baigner = to bathe, so a bathing room

La douche est-elle à droite ou à gauche
          is   it

dans l'image? La douche est

_____.
(?)

Où est le W.C. dans l'image? Le W.C. est au milieu, entre _____ **et** _____.
                                          (oh) (mill-yuh) (ah$^{(n)}$-truh)
               in the middle   between   (?)   (?)

Où est le lavabo en haut?   Le lavabo est à _____.
                                                 (?)

Où est le miroir en haut?   Le miroir est au-dessus du _____ _lavabo_ _____.
                                                       (?)

Où sont les serviettes dans l'image en haut?

Les serviettes sont au-dessus du _____. **Les serviettes sont sur** _____.
                                            (?)   (?)

Remember, **la salle de bain** means a room to bathe in. If **vous êtes dans un restaurant**
             (salle)   _(baigner)_   _(et)_
                                                            are
                                     (kah-bee-nay)   _(twah-let)_

et vous avez besoin du lavatory, **vous** want to ask for **les cabinets ou les toilettes** _not_ for
        need

la salle de bain.

Excusez-moi. Où sont les cabinets?

Restrooms fall **sous** the title of **les toilettes et** they are marked ☐D **et** ☐M . **Vous** will have a sharp surprise if **vous** think the letters stand **pour** "Dudes" **et** "Misses".

☐D **représente Dames** **et** ☐M **représente Messieurs.**
            ladies   gentlemen

☐ **le président** _(pray-zee-dah$^{(n)}$)_ .... president   _____
☐ **la presse** _(press)_ .... press, media   _____
☐ **le prix** _(pree)_ .... price, prize   _____
☐ **le problème** _(proh-blem)_ .... problem   _____
☐ **le programme** _(proh-grahm)_ .... program   _____

Next stop — **le bureau**, *(bew-row)* specifically **la table ou le bureau dans le**

bureau! **Qu'est-ce** *(kess)* **qu'il y a sur le bureau?** *(kee-lee-yah)* Let's identify **les choses** which one

normally finds **dans le bureau ou** strewn about **la maison**.

(kray-yoh(n))
le crayon

(stee-low)
le stylo

(pah-pee-ay)
le papier

(leh-truh)
la lettre

   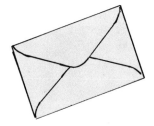

—————————— —————————— —————————— ——————————

le papier

(kart) (pohs-tall)
la carte postale

(ta(n)-bruh-post)
le timbre-poste

(lee-vruh)
le livre

(ruh-vew) (mahg-ah-zeen)
la revue/le magazine

—————————— —————————— —————————— ——————————

(zhoor-nahl)
le journal

(lew-net)
les lunettes

(tay-lay-vee-zuhr)
la téléviseur

(kor-bay) (pah-pee-ay)
la corbeille à papier

—————————— —————————— —————————— ——————————

Maintenant, label these **choses dans le bureau avec** your stickers.   Do not forget to say these **mots** out loud whenever **vous les écrivez, vous** see them **ou vous** apply the stickers.

(lay) *(zay-kree-vay)*
them   write

Maintenant, identify **les choses en bas** by filling in each blank **avec le mot correct en français.**

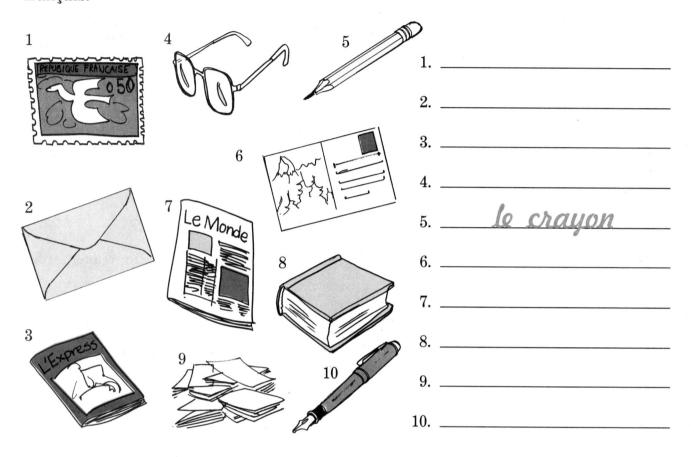

1. _____

2. _____

3. _____

4. _____

5. *le crayon*

6. _____

7. _____

8. _____

9. _____

10. _____

Voilà quatre verbes de plus.
(plews)
more

(vwahr)	*(ah(n)-vwhy-ay)*	*(door-meer)*	*(troo-vay)*
voir = to see	**envoyer** = to send	**dormir** = to sleep	**trouver** = to find

_____   _____   *dormir*   _____

Maintenant, fill in the blanks, **à la prochaine page, avec la forme correcte** of these
(pro-shen)   *(form)*
on   next   form

verbes.   Practice saying the sentences out loud many times.

☐ **le raisin** *(ray-za(n))* . . . .   grape   _____
   — le raisin sec *(sek)* . . . .   raisin (dried grape)   _____
☐ **la recette** *(ruh-set)* . . . .   recipe, receipt   _____
☐ **la récréation** *(ray-kray-ah-see-oh(n))* . . . .   recreation   _____
☐ **la région** *(ray-zhee-oh(n))* . . . .   region, area   _____

voir

Je _vois/_ _____ le lit.

Il _voit/_ _____ la couverture.
Elle

Nous _voyons/_ _____ l'hôtel.

Vous _voyez/_ _____ la Tour Eiffel.

Ils _voient/_ _____ la douche.
Elles

envoyer

J' _envoie/_ _____ la lettre.

Il _envoie/_ _____ la carte postale.
Elle

Nous _____ le livre.

Vous _____ quatre cartes postales.

Ils _envoient/_ _____ trois lettres.
Elles

dormir

Je _dors/_ _____ dans la chambre.

Il _dort/_ _____ dans le lit.
Elle

Nous _____ dans l'hôtel.

Vous _____ dans la maison.

Ils _____ sous la couverture.
Elles

trouver

Je _____ le timbre.

Il _____ les journaux.
Elle

Nous _____ les lunettes.

Vous _____ le Louvre.

Ils _____ les fleurs.
Elles

Remember that **"oi"** sounds like "wah." Practice **bois** *(bwah)* drink, **vois** *(vwah)* see, **voient** *(vwah)* see, **envoie** *(ah[n]-vwah)* sends and **envoient** *(ah[n]-vwah)* send. Also, **"ent"** at the end of a verb is silent: **trouve** *(troov)* finds and **trouvent** *(troov)* find.

The expression **n'est-ce pas** *(ness-pah)* is **extrêmement** *(ek-strem-uh-mah[n])* extremely useful **en français.** Added onto a sentence,

it turns the sentence into a question for which **la réponse** is usually **"oui."** It has only

one form and is much simpler than **en anglais.**

C'est un livre, n'est-ce pas? *(ness-pah)*	=	It's a book, isn't it?
Jacqueline est belle, n'est-ce pas?	=	Jacqueline is beautiful, isn't she?
Vous êtes français, n'est-ce pas?	=	You're French, aren't you?

Step 15

Vous know **maintenant** how to count, how to ask **questions,** how to use **verbes avec** the

"plug-in" formula, how to make statements, **et** how to describe something, be it the

location of **un hôtel ou la couleur d'une maison.** *(dewn)* *(of a)* Let's now take the basics that **vous** *(voo)*

avez *(zah-vay)* learned **et** expand them in special areas that will be most helpful in your travels.

What does everyone do on a holiday? Send postcards, **n'est-ce-pas?** *(ness-pah)* Let's learn exactly

how **le bureau de poste français (P.T.T.)** *(bew-row)* *(post)* works.
post office

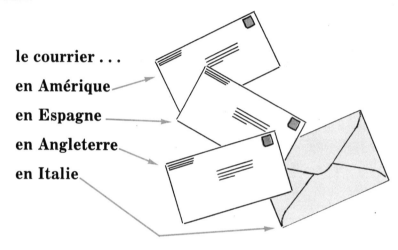

le courrier . . .

en Amérique

en Espagne

en Angleterre

en Italie

Les P.T.T. *(lay)* *(pay-tay-tay)* **(Postes, Télécommunications et Télédiffusion)** is where you need to go **en**
post office

France to buy a stamp, mail a package, send a telegram or use the telephone. **Voilà** some

mots nécessaires pour le bureau de poste. *(nay-say-sair)*
necessary

la lettre	la carte postale	le timbre-poste *(ta(n)-bruh-pohst)*	le télégramme *(tay-lay-grahm)*

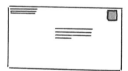   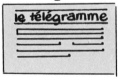

la lettre _____ _____ _____

☐ **la résidence** *(ray-zee-dah(n)s)* .... residence _____
☐ **la résistance** *(ray-zee-stah(n)s)* .... resistance _____
☐ **la révolution** *(ray-voh-lew-see-oh(n))* .... revolution _____
  — 1789 - **la Révolution française** .... French Revolution _____
☐ **la route** *(root)* .... route, highway

(pah-kay) *(koh-lee)*
le paquet/le colis

(bwaht) *(oh)* *(let-ruh)*
la boîte aux lettres

(par) *(ah-vee-oh^{(n)})*
par avion

PAR AVION
AIR MAIL

(ge-shay)
le guichet
window/counter

par avion

_____   _____   *par avion* _____

(kah-bean) *(tay-lay-phone-eek)*
la cabine téléphonique

(tay-lay-phone)
le téléphone

(pay-tay-tay) *(bew-row)*
les P.T.T./le bureau de poste

_____   _____   _____

Les P.T.T. en France ont tout. *(oh^{(n)})* *(too)* has everything **Vous envoyez** *(ah^{(n)}-vwhy-ay)* send **les télégrammes, les lettres et les cartes**

postales *(dew)* **du bureau de poste.** from the **Vous achetez les timbres dans le bureau de poste. Vous**

téléphonez *(tay-lay-phone-ay)* telephone **du bureau de poste. Le bureau de poste est généralement** *(zhay-nay-rahl-mah^{(n)})* generally open from 8:00

du matin à 7:00 du soir weekdays **et 8:00 à 12:00 le samedi.** *(sahm-dee)* Saturday If **vous avez besoin** need to call

home **en Amérique,** this can be done **au bureau de poste et** at the is called **un appel téléphonique** *(ah-pel)* call

interurbain. *(a^{(n)}-tair-ewr-ba^{(n)})* long distance Okay. First step — **entrez dans les P.T.T.**

The following **est une bonne** *(bun)* sample **conversation.** Familiarize yourself **avec ces mots** *(say)* these

maintenant.

GUICHET 7

Excusez-moi.
Où achète-t-on
des timbres?

Au guichet
numéro 7.

☐ **le sac** *(sack)* . . . . sack _____
☐ **sacré** *(sah-kray)* . . . . sacred _____
 — **Sacré-Coeur à Paris** *(sah-kray kur)* . . . . . . Sacred Heart in Paris _____
☐ **sage** *(sahzh)* . . . . wise, well-behaved _____
☐ **la saison** *(say-zoh^{(n)})* . . . . season _____

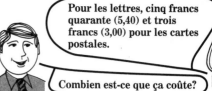

Je voudrais des timbres pour deux lettres pour l'Amérique et aussi des timbres pour deux cartes postales pour l'Amérique.

Par avion?

Pour les lettres, cinq francs quarante (5,40) et trois francs (3,00) pour les cartes postales.

Combien est-ce que ça coûte?

Oui, par avion, s'il vous plaît. Je voudrais aussi des timbres pour deux lettres pour la France. Combien est-ce?

Un franc soixante (1,60).

Bon

Voilà les timbres. Ça fait dix francs (10F).

Merci bien, Madame.

Next step — **vous** ask **questions** like those **en bas** depending upon what **vous voudriez.** *(voo-dree-ay)* want

Où est-ce qu'on achète des timbres? *(ess) (koh$^{(n)}$) (nah-shet)* one buy

Où est-ce qu'on envoie un télégramme? *(ess) (koh$^{(n)}$) (nah$^{(n)}$-vwah)*

Où est-ce qu'on achète une carte postale?

Où est-ce qu'on envoie un paquet?

Où est-ce qu'on téléphone?

Où est la cabine téléphonique? *(ay)*

Où est-ce qu'on fait un appel téléphonique interurbain? *(ah-pel)* call *(a$^{(n)}$-tair-ewr-ba$^{(n)}$)* long distance

Où est-ce qu'on fait un appel téléphonique local? *(low-kahl)*

Combien est-ce que ça coûte?

Répétez many times **ces phrases en haut.** **Maintenant,** quiz yourself. See if **vous** can translate *(say) (frahz)* these sentences

the following thoughts **en français.** **Les réponses sont en bas de la prochaine page.** *(pro-shen)* next

1. Where is the telephone booth?_____

2. Where does one make a phone call?_____

3. Where does one make a local phone call?_____

4. Where does one make a long-distance phone call?_____

5. Where is the post office?_____

☐ **la salutation** *(sah-lew-tah-see-oh$^{(n)}$)* . . . . greeting _____

☐ **le sandwich** *(sah$^{(n)}$-dweech)* . . . . sandwich _____

☐ **la sauce** *(sohs)* . . . . sauce _____

☐ **le saumon** *(soh-moh$^{(n)}$)* . . . . salmon _____

☐ **la science** *(see-ah$^{(n)}$s)* . . . . science _____

62

6. Where does one buy stamps?_____

7. How much is it?_____

8. Where does one send a package?_____

9. Where does one send a telegram?_____

10. Where is window eight?_____

Voilà quatre nouveaux verbes.

(fare) **faire** = to do/make   *(moh⁽ⁿ⁾-tray)* **montrer** = to show   *(ay-kreer)* **écrire** = to write   *(pay-yay)* **payer** = to pay

_____   _____   *écrire* _____

faire

Je *fais/* _____ un appel téléphonique.

Il
Elle *fait/* _____ le *(lee)* **lit.**
                                    bed

Nous *faisons/* _____ beaucoup.
                              a lot

Vous ne *faites/* _____ *(ree-a⁽ⁿ⁾)* **rien.**
                                    nothing

Ils
Elles *font/* _____ *(too)* **tout.**
                              everything

montrer

Je vous *montre/* _____ le livre.

Il   vous _____ le bureau.
Elle to you

Nous vous _____ le château.
     to you   castle

(muh)
Vous me _____ la lettre.
     to me

Ils   me _____ les P.T.T.
Elles to me

écrire

J' *écris/* _____ une lettre.

Il
Elle *écrit/* _____ beaucoup.

Nous *écrivons/* _____ un télégramme.

Vous _____ *(voh-truh)* votre *(seen-yah-tewr)* signature.
                          your   signature

Ils
Elles n' *écrivent/* _____ rien.

payer

Je *paie/* _____ *(lah-dee-see-oh⁽ⁿ⁾)* **l'addition.**
                                    bill in restaurant

Ils
Elles *paie/* _____ la **taxe.**
                              tax

Nous *payons/* _____ la **note.**
                              bill in hotel

(pree)
Vous _____ le **prix.**
                    price

Ils
Elles ne *paient/* _____ rien.

63

Step 16

(ko-mah⁽ⁿ⁾)   *(pay-yay)*
Comment payer
how   to pay

Oui, il y a aussi bills to pay **en France.** **Vous** have just finished your **repas délicieux** *(ruh-pah) (day-lee-see-yuh)*
there are   also   meal   delicious

et vous voudriez l'addition et vous voudriez payer. **Que faites-vous?** **Vous** call for *(fet)*
bill   do you do

(sair-vur)   *(gar-soh⁽ⁿ⁾)*   *(sair-vuz)*
le serveur (**le garçon**) **ou la serveuse.**
waiter   waitress

> **Excusez-moi. Je voudrais l'addition, s'il vous plaît.**

> **Bien sûr, Monsieur. Une minute.**

Le serveur will normally reel off what **vous** *(voo)*

avez eaten, while writing rapidly. **Il** will then *(zah-vay)*

place **une petite feuille de papier sur la** *(puh-teet) (fuh-yuh)*
little   sheet

table that looks like **l'addition dans l'image,**

while saying something like:

(fay)   *(muh-see-uh)*
"Ça fait vingt-six francs soixante, Monsieur."
makes

Vous will pay **le serveur** or perhaps **vous** will pay **à la caisse.** Tipping **en France est** *(kess)*
at   cashier

généralement much easier than **en Amérique.** If your bill or the menu is marked

(sair-vees)   *(koh⁽ⁿ⁾-pree)*
"Service compris," then your tip has already been included in your bill. If not, then a
service   included

> **Un dîner excellent. Merci.**

> *(eel-nee-ah) (pah)*   *(kwah)*
> **Il n'y a pas de quoi.**
> you're welcome
>
> **Au revoir, Monsieur.**

15% tip left **sur la table** is customary. Most

French eating establishments are **"Service**

compris," but don't forget to look. You

might find some that are **"Service non**
not

compris."

Remember these key **mots** when dining out **à la française.** *(frah⁽ⁿ⁾-sez)*
in the French manner

(muh-new) **le menu** or *(kart)* **la carte**	*(poor-bwahr)* **le pourboire** tip
(lah-dee-see-oh⁽ⁿ⁾) **l'addition**	**service compris**

(poh-lee-tess)
La politesse est très importante en France. You will feel more **français** if you practice
politeness

(say) (zek-spreh-see-oh⁽ⁿ⁾)
and use **ces expressions.** **excusez-moi** or **pardon**
these expressions

s'il vous plaît   *(boh-koo)* **merci beaucoup** or **merci bien** *(bee-a⁽ⁿ⁾)*   *(eel)(nee-ah) (pah) (duh)(kwah)* **il n'y a pas de quoi**
you're welcome/it's nothing

Voilà une sample **conversation** involving paying **la note** *(note)* when leaving **un hôtel.**
bill

Jeannette: **Excusez-moi, Monsieur. Voudriez-vous me préparer la note?**
(voo-dree-ay-voo) (muh) (pray-pah-ray)
would   you   for me prepare

(low-tell-ee-ay) *(kel)*
L'Hôtelier: **Quelle chambre, s'il vous plaît?**
hotelkeeper   what

Jeannette: **Numéro trois cent dix.**

L'Hôtelier: **Merci. Une minute, s'il vous plaît.**

L'Hôtelier: **Voilà la note. Ça fait quatre-vingt-dix francs vingt.**

Jeannette: **Merci beaucoup (et Jeannette** hands him **un billet de cent francs.**

L'Hôtelier returns shortly **et dit)** *(dee)*
says

(voh-truh)(ruh-sue) *(oh) (ruh-vwahr)*
L'Hôtelier: **Voilà votre reçu et votre monnaie. Merci et au revoir.**
your   receipt   money   good-bye

Simple, right? If **vous avez** any **problème avec les nombres,** just ask the person to write

(sohm)
out **la somme** so that **vous** can be sure you understand everything correctly.
sum

(ay-kree-vay-mwah)
"S'il vous plaît, écrivez-moi la somme. Merci."
write   for me   sum

Let's take a break from **l'argent et,** starting **à la prochaine page,** learn some **nouveaux**

fun **mots.**

- ☐ **le ski** *(ski)* .... skiing _____
- — **le ski-nautique** *(ski-no-teek)* .... water skiing _____
- ☐ **la Sorbonne** *(sore-bun)* .... part of University of Paris _____
- ☐ **la soupe** *(soup)* .... soup _____
- ☐ **le spectacle** *(spek-tah-kluh)* .... spectacle, performance _____

65

Il est en bonne forme.   **Il est malade.**   *(mah-lahd)*   C'est **bon.**   *(boh⁽ⁿ⁾)*

sick   good

(suh) (nay) (pah) (boh⁽ⁿ⁾)
Ce n'est pas bon.
not

(mow-vay)
C'est **mauvais.**
bad

(showd)
L'eau est **chaude.**
warm

Elle a 50 degrés.

do not *(fwahd)*
L'eau est **froide.**
cold

Elle a 17 degrés.

(for)
Vous parlez **fort.**
loudly

(deuce-mah⁽ⁿ⁾)
Nous parlons **doucement.**
softly

(koort)
La ligne rouge est **courte.**

(lohng)
La ligne bleue est **longue.**

La femme est **grande.**

L'enfant est **petite.**

en haut

à gauche   à droite

en bas

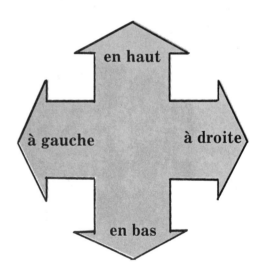

(grow)
Le livre rouge est **gros.**
thick

(ma⁽ⁿ⁾s)
Le livre vert est **mince.**
thin

(ah) (luhr)
20 kilomètres à l'heure
per hour

200 kilomètres à l'heure

(lah⁽ⁿ⁾)
lent
slow

(veet) (rah-peed)
vite/rapide
fast

66

Les montagnes sont hautes. *(moh(n)-tahn-yah) (oht)* Elles ont 2000 mètres de haut. *(meh-truh)*
mountains · high · have · meters

Les montagnes sont basses. *(bahs)* Elles ont seulement 800 mètres de haut.
low

Le grand-père est vieux. *(vee-yuh)* Il a soixante-dix ans. *(ah(n))*
old · has · years

L'enfant est jeune. *(zhun)* Il a seulement dix ans.
young

La chambre d'hôtel est chère. *(share)* Elle coûte 994F50.
expensive

La chambre de l'AJ est bon marché. *(lah-zhee) (boh(n))(mar-shay)* Elle coûte 130F50.
youth hostel · inexpensive

J'ai 2.000F. Je suis **riche.** *(reesh)* C'est **beaucoup** d'argent. *(boh-koo)*
rich · a lot

Il a seulement 4F. Il est **pauvre.** *(poh-vruh)* C'est **peu** d'argent. *(puh)*
poor · little

Voilà de nouveaux verbes.
some

(sah-vwahr)	*(poo-vwahr)*	*(duh-vwahr)*	*(leer)*
savoir = to know (a fact, an address, etc.)	**pouvoir** = to be able to/can	**devoir** = to have to/ must/to owe	**lire** = to read

_____ _____ _devoir_____ _____

Les verbes "savoir," "pouvoir" et "devoir," along with **le verbe "vouloir,"** can be joined

with another **verbe:**

nous savons trouver l'adresse
know how · to find

nous savons parler français

nous pouvons parler
can · speak

nous pouvons comprendre
understand

nous devons payer
must · pay

nous devons manger
eat

☐ **supérieur** *(sue-pay-ree-ur)* .... superior, upper
☐ **la surprise** *(sewr-preez)* .... surprise
☐ **sympathique** *(sa(n)-pah-teek)* .... likeable, nice
  — Qu'il est sympa! *(kee-lay sa(n)-pah)* ..... Oh, he's so nice.
☐ **le système** *(see-stem)* .... system

Study their pattern closely as **vous** will use **beaucoup de ces verbes.**
a lot   (say)
these

savoir

Je _sais/_____ tout.
everything

Ils _sait/_____l'adresse.
Elle
Nous _savons/_____ parler français.

Vous _____ commander une bière.

Ils   ne _savent/_____ pas l'adresse.
Elles^(do not)

pouvoir

Je _peux/_____ parler français.

Ils _peut/_____ comprendre l'anglais.
Elle
Nous _pouvons/_____boire.

Vous _____entrer.

Ils _peuvent/_____ parler français aussi.
Elles

devoir

Je_dois/_____ payer la note.

Ils _doit/_____ rester à l'hôtel.
Elle
Nous _devons/_____ visiter Paris.

Vous nous _devez/_____ 5 francs.
to us

Ils _doivent/_____ payer l'addition.
Elles

lire

Je _lis/_____ le livre.

Ils _lit/_____ le journal.
Elle
Nous _lisons/_____ le menu.

Vous _____ beaucoup.

Ils _lisent/_____ tout.
Elles

Pouvez-vous translate these thoughts **en bas en français?   Les réponses sont en bas.**

1.   I can speak French. _____

2.   He must pay now. _____

3.   We don't know the address. _____

4.   You owe us ten francs. _____

5.   She knows everything. _____

6.   I am able to speak a little French. _____

Maintenant, draw **des lignes entre** the opposites **en bas.** Don't forget to say them out
(leen-yuh)

loud. Use **ces mots** every day to describe **les choses dans votre maison, dans votre**
(voh-truh)
your

(ay-kohl)
école, at work, etc.
school

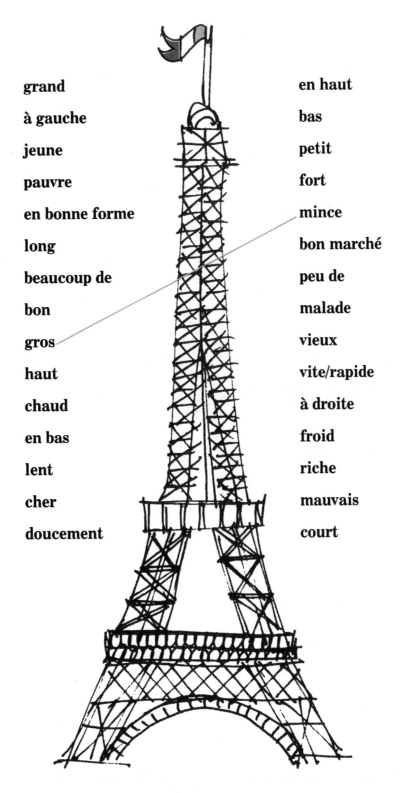

grand	en haut
à gauche	bas
jeune	petit
pauvre	fort
en bonne forme	mince
long	bon marché
beaucoup de	peu de
bon	malade
gros	vieux
haut	vite/rapide
chaud	à droite
en bas	froid
lent	riche
cher	mauvais
doucement	court

☐ **le tabac** *(tah-bah)* . . . . tobacco _____
— **le bureau de tabac** . . . . tobacco shop _____
☐ **la tapisserie** *(tah-pee-suh-ree)* . . . . tapestry, wall-paper _____
☐ **le tarif** *(tah-reef)* . . . . tariff, fare _____
☐ **le tennis** *(teh-nees)* . . . . tennis _____

Step 17

Le Voyageur Voyage
(vwhy-ah-zhur) traveler   *(vwhy-ahzh)* travels

Hier à Bordeaux!   **Aujourd'hui à Tours!**   **Demain à Paris!**

Lundi à Dijon!   **Mercredi à Marseille!**   **Vendredi à Nice!**

Traveling **est** easy, clean, **et** efficient **en France.** La France n'est pas très grande, in fact, it is slightly smaller than the state of Texas. *(doh*$^{(n)}$*k)* therefore **Donc, le voyage est très facile** *(fah-seal)* easy within the inviting hexagon *(key)* which *(sah-pel)* is called **qui s'appelle la "France."** **Comment voyager en France?**

Etienne voyage en auto.    **Colette voyage en train.**

Françoise voyage en avion.    **Marie-Anne voyage en bateau.**

Xavier et Lucette voyagent à bicyclette à travers la France.
across

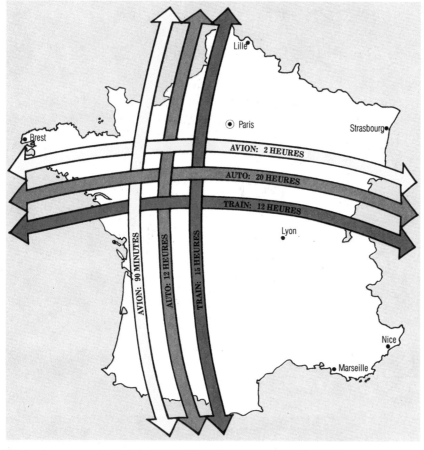

Regardez la carte à gauche. C'est la France, *(ness-pah)* n'est-ce pas? Pour voyager du nord au sud, il faut seulement 90 minutes en avion, 12 heures en auto et 15 heures en train. *(pah)* **Pas** not *(mah)* **mal,** n'est-ce pas? bad

☐ **la terrasse** *(tay-rahs)* . . . . terrace, sidewalk cafe
☐ **thermal** *(tair-mahl)* . . . . thermal
  — les eaux thermales *(lay-zoh)* . . . . hot springs
☐ **le théâtre** *(tay-ah-truh)* . . . . theater
☐ **le ticket** *(tee-kay)* . . . . ticket, check

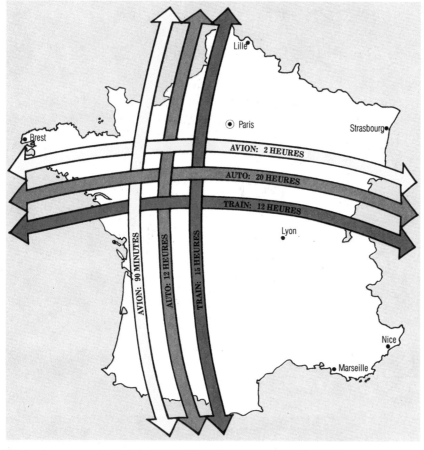

Les Français adorent voyager, *(ah-door)* *(sewr-preez)* so it is no **surprise** to find **beaucoup de mots** built on **le**
love · to travel

mot "voyage" *(vwhy-ahzh)* which means "journey" or "trip." Practice saying **les mots suivants** many

times. **Vous** will see them **souvent.** *(soo-vah(n))*
often

voyager

faire un voyage
to take a trip

le voyageur
traveler

voyager en avion

voyager en bateau

voyager en auto

voyager en train

voyager en autobus

voyager à bicyclette   **voyager à pied** *(ah)(pee-ay)*   **une agence de voyage** *(ah-zhah(n)s)*   **bon voyage!**
on · foot   travel agency   have a good trip

En bas il y a some basic signs which **vous devez** *(duh-vay)* also learn to recognize quickly. Most of
should

ces mots come from **les verbes** **entrer** *(ah(n)-tray)* = to enter **et** **sortir** *(sor-teer)* = to go out.

ENTRÉE

SORTIE

l'entrée *(lah(n)-tray)* _____
entrance

l'entrée principale *(pra(n)-see-pahl)* _____
main entrance

l'entrée latérale *(lah-tay-rahl)* _____
side entrance

la sortie *(sor-tee)* *la sortie*
exit

la sortie principale _____   **défense d'entrer** *(day-fah(n)s)(dah(n)-tray)* _____
main exit   do not enter

la sortie de secours *(suh-koor)* _____   **entrée interdite** *(a(n)-tair-deet)* _____
emergency exit   do not enter

☐ **le tour** *(tour)* . . . . circumference, tour _____
  — **Le Tour de France** . . . . bicycle race in France _____
☐ **la tour** *(tour)* . . . . tower _____
☐ **tricolore** *(tree-ko-lor)* . . . . tricolored _____
  — **le drapeau tricolore** *(drah-poh)* . . . . French flag **(bleu, blanc, rouge)** _____ 71

(ah-lay)
Aller est un verbe très important pour le **voyageur**. If you choose to **aller en automobile,**
to go   *(vwhy-ah-zhur)*
                                                                              traveler

here are a few key **mots.**

(low-toe-root)
l'autoroute_____
highway

(koh$^{(n)}$-trah-vah$^{(n)}$-see-oh$^{(n)}$)
une contravention _____
parking ticket

(root)
la route à Avignon _____
road   to Avignon

(vwah-tewr)   *(loo-ay)*
une voiture à louer _____
rental car

(ah-zhah$^{(n)}$s)   *(low-kah-see-oh$^{(n)}$)*   *(vwah-tewr)*
une agence de location   de voitures _____
car-rental agency

Voilà quatre opposites **très importants.**

PARIS-ORLEANS-TOURS-BORDEAUX

(lah-ree-vay)
l'arrivée _____
arrival

(day-par)
le départ _____ *le départ*
departure

(lay-trah$^{(n)}$-zhay)
à l'étranger _____
foreign

(la$^{(n)}$-tay-ree-ur)
à l'intérieur _____
domestic

(vwhy-ahzh)
Let's learn the basic **verbes de voyage.** Follow the same pattern as you have in previous Steps.

(prah$^{(n)}$-druh) *(lah-vee-oh$^{(n)}$)*
prendre l'avion = to take
                   a plane/
                   to fly

(ah-tair-ear)
atterrir = to land

(ray-zair-vay)
réserver = to reserve/to book

_____

                   atterrir

_____

(ah-ree-vay)
arriver = to arrive

(par-teer)
partir = to leave

(koh$^{(n)}$-dweer)
conduire = to drive

_____

_____

_____

(moh$^{(n)}$-tay)
monter = to board/
              to climb into

(day-bar-kay)
débarquer = to disembark/
                to get out

(shah$^{(n)}$-zhay)
changer de train = to
                  transfer (trains)

_____

☐ **unique** *(ew-neek)* . . . . sole, only, single _____
  — **enfant unique** *(ah$^{(n)}$-fah$^{(n)}$ tew-neek)* . . . only child _____
☐ **universel** *(ew-nee-vair-sell)* . . . . universal _____
☐ **l'université** *(lew-nee-vair-see-tay)* . . . . university _____
72 ☐ **l'urgence** *(lewr-zhah$^{(n)}$s)*. . . . . urgency

Avec ces verbes, vous êtes *(et)* ready for any **voyage** anywhere. **Vous** should have no

problèmes avec les verbes, just remember the basic "plug in" formula **nous** learned

already. Use that knowledge to translate the following thoughts **en français. Les**

réponses sont en bas.

1. I fly to Paris. _____

2. I transfer trains in Toulon. _____

3. He lands in Marseille. _____

4. We arrive tomorrow. _____

5. You get off in Tours. _____

6. They travel to Strasbourg. _____

7. Where is the train to Lyon? _____

8. How can one go to Switzerland? With TWA or Air France? _____

_____

Voilà de nouveaux mots pour votre voyage. As always, write out **les mots et** practice
some
the sample **phrases** *(frahz)* out loud.
sentences

(kay)
le quai
platform

(gar)
la gare
train station

(lah-ay-row-por)
l'aéroport
airport

_____

**Pardon. Où est le quai
numéro deux?**

_____

Pardon. Où est la gare?

_____

Pardon. Où est l'aéroport?

(bew-row) *(shah⁽ⁿ⁾zh)*

le bureau de change
money-exchange office

LE BUREAU DE CHANGE

(day) *(zohb-zhay)* *(troo-vay)*

le bureau des objets trouvés
lost-and-found office

LE BUREAU DES OBJETS TROUVÉS

(low-rare) *(ess-n-say-ef)*

l'horaire (de SNCF)
timetable of French railroad

PARIS-ORLEANS-TOURS													
0	Paris (Austerlitz) .... dep.	6 15	..	..	6	457	057	508	038	379	00		
119	Les Aubrais .... arr.		..	..		8 10		9 00					
121	Orléans .... { arr.	7 17	..	..			8 20		9 08				
	{ dep.	7 23	..	7 46			8 06		8 51				
119	Les Aubrais .... dep.		..		7 57		8 14		9 02				
173	Blois .... dep.	7 54	..		8 37		8 47						
210	Ambroise .... dep.		..		8 58								
232	St. Pierre-des-Corps . arr.	8 20	..		9 098	289	159	239	52	1034			
235	Tours .... { arr.	8 27	..	9 168	379	229	31	1001	1046				
	{ dep.		6 06		8 10	..	9	159	45	1024				

Pardon. Où est le bureau de change?

Pardon. Où est le bureau des objets trouvés?

Pardon. Où est l'horaire?

(oh-kew-pay)

occupé (une place occupée) _____
occupied

(lee-bruh)

libre _____
free

(koh⁽ⁿ⁾-par-tuh-mah⁽ⁿ⁾)

le compartiment _____
compartment

(plahs)

la place _____ *la place*
seat

(set)   *(ay-tell)*

Cette place est-elle occupée? _____
this   is   it

Cette place est-elle libre? _____

(suh)   *(ay-teel)*

Ce compartiment est-il occupé? _____
this   is   it

Ce compartiment est-il libre? _____

Practice writing out **les questions suivantes.** It will help you *(plew)* *(tar)* **plus tard.**
later

Excusez-moi. Où sont les toilettes? _____

(vah-goh⁽ⁿ⁾) *(res-toe-rah⁽ⁿ⁾)*

Excusez-moi. Où est le wagon-restaurant? _____
dining car

(sahl) *(dah-tah⁽ⁿ⁾t)*

Où est la salle d'attente? _____ *Où est la salle d'attente?*
room   waiting

(ge-shay)

Où est le guichet numéro huit? _____

(a⁽ⁿ⁾-tair-dee) *(few-may)*

Est-ce interdit de fumer? _____
is it prohibited   to smoke

☐ **les vacances** *(vah-kah⁽ⁿ⁾s)* .... vacation, holidays _____
  —**les grandes vacances**.............. summer vacation _____
☐ **la valse** *(valse)* .... waltz _____
☐ **la vanille** *(vah-nee-yuh)* .... vanilla _____
  —**la glace à la vanille** *(glahs)* .... vanilla ice cream

Increase your **mots des voyage** by writing out **les mots en bas et** practicing the sample

(frahz)
phrases out loud.
sentences

(ah)
à _____
to
         Le train est-il à Paris?

(vwah)
la voie_____
track
      Le train part de la voie numéro sept.

(koh⁽ⁿ⁾-seen-yuh)
la consigne _____
left-luggage office

(por-tur)
le porteur_____
porter

(tah⁽ⁿ⁾)
temps _____
time
        J'ai très peu de temps.

(rah⁽ⁿ⁾-sen-yuh-mah⁽ⁿ⁾)
le bureau de renseignements _____
information bureau

_____
   Où est le bureau de renseignements?

(bee-ay)
le billet   *le billet, le billet*
airplane/train ticket

Practice **ces mots** every day.   **Vous** will be surprised how **souvent vous** will use them.
(soo-vah⁽ⁿ⁾)
often

Pouvez-vous lire la leçon suivante?

(et)   *(ah-see)*
Vous êtes maintenant assis dans l'avion et vous allez en France.   **Vous avez exchanged**
        seated

de l'argent (you have, haven't you?), **vous avez les billets et le passeport et vous avez les**

(vah-leez)   *(ah-tair-ee-say)*
valises all packed.   **Vous êtes maintenant touriste.**   **Vous atterrissez demain à 14:15 en**
suitcases

             (bee-ya⁽ⁿ⁾)
France.   **Bon voyage!**   **Amusez-vous bien.**
             well

Maintenant, vous have arrived **et vous** head for **la gare** in order to get to **votre**

(day-stee-nah-see-oh⁽ⁿ⁾)(fee-nahl)
destination   **finale.**   **Les trains français** come in many shapes, sizes **et** speeds.   **Il y a**

(rah-peed)   *(lek-spress)*   *(lome-nee-boos)*   *(low-toe-rye)*
le rapide (très rapide), **l'express** (assez rapide), **l'omnibus** (lent) **et l'autorail** (aussi
                  fairly

           (oh⁽ⁿ⁾)   *(vah-goh⁽ⁿ⁾)*   *(vah-goh⁽ⁿ⁾-lee)*
lent).   Some **trains ont un wagon-restaurant et** some **trains ont un wagon-lit ou des**
             have   dining car   sleeping car

(koo-shet)
couchettes.   All this will be indicated **sur l'horaire,** but remember **vous savez comment**
berths

                                (koh⁽ⁿ⁾-bee-nay-zoh⁽ⁿ⁾)
to ask things like this.   Practice your possible **combinaisons de questions** by writing out
                                combinations

the following samples.

Y a-t-il un wagon-restaurant dans le train? _____
is   there

Y a-t-il des couchettes dans le train? *Y a-t-il* _____

Y a-t-il un wagon-lit dans le train? _____

☐ **la variété** *(vah-ree-ay-tay)* . . . . variety   _____
☐ **la veine** *(ven)* . . . . vein (in the body)   _____
  — **avoir de la veine** . . . . to be lucky   _____
☐ **la version** *(vair-see-oh⁽ⁿ⁾)* . . . . version, film translation   _____
  — **la version originale (VO)** *(oh-ree-zhee-nahl)* . . original version (of a film)   _____ **75**

What about inquiring about **le prix des billets ou le tarif?** *(pree)* *(bee-ay)* *(tah-reef)* **Vous pouvez formuler des** *(for-mew-lay)* questions.

price — tickets — fare — formulate

(kohm-bee-yen)
Combien est le billet (le tarif) pour Bayonne? _____ *(by-own)*

(ah-lay)
aller _____ *aller, aller* _____ **aller et retour** _____ *(ruh-tour)*
one-way — round-trip

Combien est le billet pour Bordeaux? _____ *(bore-doe)*

Combien est le billet pour Lille? _____ *(leel)*

Aller ou aller et retour? _____

What about times of **départs et arrivées?** *(day-par)* *(ah-ree-vay)* **Vous pouvez formuler ces questions aussi.**
departures — arrivals

À quelle heure part le train pour Grenoble? *À quelle* _____ *(gruh-noh-bluh)*
leaves

À quelle heure part l'avion pour Rome? _____

À quelle heure arrive le train de Madrid? _____ *(mah-dreed)*
from

À quelle heure arrive l'Àvion de New York? _____

Vous have arrived **en France. Vous êtes maintenant à la gare. Où voudriez-vous** *(voo-dree-ay-voo)*
at the — would you like

(zah-lay)
aller? Well, tell that to the person at the **guichet** selling **les billets.** *(bee-ay)*

Je voudrais aller en Bretagne. _____ *(bruh-tahn-yuh)*

Je voudrais aller à Aix-en-Provence. _____ *(eks-ah[n]-pro-vah[n]s)*

Nous voudrions aller à Versailles. *Nous voudrions aller à Versailles.* *(vair-sigh)*

À quelle heure part le train pour Nice? _____

Combien coûte le billet pour Versailles? _____

Je voudrais un billet pour Versailles. _____

(pruh-mee-air) *(klahs)*
première classe _____ **deuxième classe** _____ *(duh-zee-em)*
first — class — second — class

Aller ou aller et retour? _____

(dwah-zh)
Dois-je changer de train? _____ **Merci.** _____
must — I

Avec this practice, **vous êtes** off **et** running. **Ces mots de voyage** will make your holiday

twice as enjoyable **et** at least three times as easy. Review **ces nouveaux mots** by doing

76 the crossword puzzle **à la page 77.** Practice drilling yourself on this Step by selecting

other locations **et** asking your own **questions** about **les trains, les autobus ou les avions** that go there. Select **de nouveaux mots de votre dictionnaire et** practice asking

questions that **commencent** *(ko-mah⁽ⁿ⁾s)* / begin **par** *(par)* / by | **OÙ** | **QUAND** | **COMBIEN** | **COMBIEN DE FOIS** *(fwah)* how often/how many times

ou making statements like **Je voudrais aller à Paris.**

Je voudrais acheter un billet.

MOTS CROISÉS

ACROSS
1. train station
2. timetable
3. track
4. yes
5. with
6. we/us
7. to smoke
8. information bureau
9. no
10. money
11. platform
12. passport
13. airport
14. free
15. to climb into/board
16. entrance

DOWN
1. to arrive
2. to change trains
3. traveler
4. good trip
5. dining car
6. to disembark
7. exit
8. to go
9. she
10. to leave
11. time
12. nothing

Step 18

Le Menu ou la Carte
(muh-new) *(kart)*
menu

Vous êtes maintenant en France et vous avez une chambre. Et maintenant? Vous

avez faim. *(fa⁽ⁿ⁾)* / have / hunger Vous voudriez manger. Mais, où y a-t-il un bon restaurant? *(may)* but / *(ee-ah-teel)* is there First of all,

il y a different types of places to eat. *(eel-ee-ah)* there are Let's learn them.

le restaurant *(res-toe-rah⁽ⁿ⁾)*	= exactly what it says, with a variety of meals **and** prices
la brasserie *(brah-suh-ree)*	= originally a beer saloon, but now also a restaurant
l'auberge *(low-bairzh)*	= originally a country inn, but it can be an inviting city restaurant
le bistro *(bee-stroh)*	= slang for **le bar** or a small, intimate restaurant with lots of atmosphere
le bar	= like a pub which serves morning pastries but concentrates on liquid refreshments
le café *(kah-fay)*	= like **le bar,** here you will find mainly drinks served (This is where you want to sip your coffee at the sidewalk table.)
le restaurant routier *(roo-tee-ay)*	= truck stop
le snack bar	= offers a quick meal of sandwiches, quiche, etc., the eating is often done standing up

Try them all. Experiment. **Vous trouvez maintenant un bon restaurant. Vous entrez**

dans le restaurant et trouvez une place. Sharing **tables avec** others **est a common et**

très pleasant **coutume en Europe.** *(koo-tewm)* custom If **vous voyez une chaise** vacant, just be sure to ask *(vwhy-ay)* see

Excusez-moi. Cette place est-elle libre?
(set) *(ay-tell)* *(lee-bruh)*
is it

If **vous avez besoin d'un menu,** catch the attention of **le serveur et** say

Monsieur! Le menu (ou la carte), s'il vous plaît.

☐ **la vierge** *(vee-airzh)*................... virgin _____
   — **la Sainte Vierge** *(sa⁽ⁿ⁾t)*............. Virgin Mary _____
☐ **la vigne** *(veen-yuh)* .... grape vine _____
☐ **le vigneron** *(veen-yur-oh⁽ⁿ⁾)* .... wine-grower _____
☐ **le vignoble** *(veen-yuh-no-bluh)*........ vineyard _____

En France, il y a trois main **repas** *(ruh-pah)* to enjoy every day, plus **un café et** perhaps **une**
(eel-ee-ah)
meals

pâtisserie pour le voyageur fatigué late in **l'après-midi.**
(pah-tee-suh-ree)
pastry

le petit déjeuner *(puh-tee) (day-zhuh-nay)*	= breakfast...	a "continental breakfast," with **café ou thé et** toast **ou croissant.** Be sure to check serving times before retiring.
le déjeuner *(day-zhuh-nay)*	= lunch.......	generally served from 12:00 to 14:00. You will be able to find any type of meal, **grand ou petit,** served at this time.
le dîner *(dee-nay)*	= dinner.....	generally served from 19:30 to 22:00. **Les Français** eat much later than Americans. This meal is meant to be relished, surrounded by good friends and a pleasant atmosphere.

If **vous** look around you **dans un restaurant français, vous** will see that some **coutumes**
(koo-tewm)
customs

françaises sont différentes from ours. **Le pain** may be set directly on the tablecloth,
(dee-fay-rah(n)t)   *(pa(n))*
bread

elbows are often rested **sur la table** and please do not forget to mop up your **sauce avec**

votre pain! **Vous** will hear **"Bon appétit"** before **votre repas et** an inquiring **"C'était**
(bun) (ah-pay-tee)   *(say-tay)*

bon?" after **vous** have finished. **Le serveur** is asking if **vous** enjoyed **votre repas et** if it

tasted good. A smile **et a "Oui, merci"** will tell him that you enjoyed it.

Maintenant, it may be **petit déjeuner** time **à Denver, mais vous êtes en France et il est**
(may)
but

19:00. Most **restaurants français** post **le menu** outside. Always read it before entering

so **vous savez** what type of **repas et prix vous** will encounter inside. Most **restaurants**
(pree)
prices

offer **un plat du jour ou un menu à prix fixe.** This is a complete **repas** at a fair **prix.** In
(plah) (dew)   fixed
special meal of the day

addition, **il y a** all the following main categories **sur le menu.**
(muh-new)

- ☐ **le village** *(vee-lahzh)*................ village _____
- ☐ **le vin** *(va(n))*...................... wine _____
- ☐ **la visite** *(vee-zeet)* .... visit _____
- ☐ **la vitamine** *(vee-tah-mean)* .... vitamin _____
- ☐ **le vocabulaire** *(voh-kah-bew-lair)* ..... vocabulary _____

79

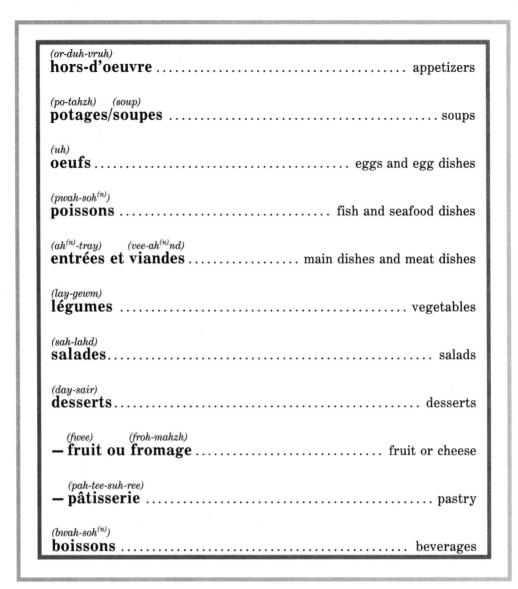

(or-duh-vruh)
hors-d'oeuvre .... appetizers

(po-tahzh) *(soup)*
potages/soupes .... soups

(uh)
oeufs .... eggs and egg dishes

(pwah-soh⁽ⁿ⁾)
poissons .... fish and seafood dishes

(ah⁽ⁿ⁾-tray) *(vee-ah⁽ⁿ⁾nd)*
entrées et viandes .... main dishes and meat dishes

(lay-gewm)
légumes .... vegetables

(sah-lahd)
salades .... salads

(day-sair)
desserts .... desserts

(fwee) *(froh-mahzh)*
— fruit ou fromage .... fruit or cheese

(pah-tee-suh-ree)
— pâtisserie .... pastry

(bwah-soh⁽ⁿ⁾)
boissons .... beverages

(spay-see-ah-lee-tay)

Most **restaurants** also offer **les specialités de la maison ou** specific meals prepared

(pahr) *(shef)*
par le chef. And if **vous** are sampling the wine, don't forget to ask about the **vin de la**
by   house wine

maison. Maintenant for a preview of delights to come ... At the back of this **livre vous**

(troo-vay)
trouvez a sample **menu français. Lisez le menu aujourd'hui et apprenez les nouveaux**

mots! Quand vous are ready to leave for **Europe,** cut out **le menu,** fold it **et** carry it in

your pocket, wallet **ou** purse. **Vous pouvez aller dans** any **restaurant et** feel prepared!
                                                         (poo-vay) *(zah-lay)*
                                                          can

Enjoy your meal! **Bon appétit!**

Most "w" words are foreign additions to **le français.**
☐ **le wagon** *(vah-goh⁽ⁿ⁾)* .... railroad car _____
☐ **le week-end** *(week-end)* .... weekend _____
☐ **le western** *(wes-tairn)* .... western (film) _____
80 ☐ **le whisky** *(we-skee)* .... whisky _____

In addition, learning the following should help you to identify what kind of meat **ou** poultry **vous commandez et comment** it will be prepared.

(buf)
boeuf
beef

(voh)
veau
veal

(ahn-yoh)
agneau
lamb

(por)
porc
pork

(voh-lie)
volaille
poultry

(zhee-bee-ay)
gibier
wild game

(kwee)
cuit = cooked

(roh-tee)
rôti = roasted

(free)
frit = fried

(kwee) (toh) (foor)
cuit au four = baked

(gree-ay)
grillé = grilled

(far-see)
farci = stuffed

(lay-gewm)
Vous will also get **légumes avec votre repas et** perhaps **une salade** *(vairt)* **verte,** after **l'entrée.**
vegetables   green

(mar-shay)
One day at an open-air **marché** will teach you **les noms** for all the different kinds of
market

(fwee)
légumes et fruits, plus it will be a delightful experience for you. **Vous pouvez** always
can

consult your menu guide at the back of **ce livre** if **vous** *(voo)* **oubliez** *(zoo-blee-ay)* **le nom correct.**
forget

(voo-dree-ay)
Maintenant vous avez decided what **vous voudriez manger et le serveur arrive.**

Et comme boisson?

Je voudrais la soupe du jour et une côtelette de porc.

Un verre de vin blanc, s'il vous plaît.

_____
_____
_____
_____
_____

81

(noo-blee-ay) *(pah)*
N'oubliez pas to treat yourself to **un dessert français.** You would not want to miss out on
don't forget

trying **les desserts suivants.**
following

(krem) *(kah-rah-mel)*
une crème caramel
custard with burnt sugar sauce

(tart) *(oh)* *(pohm)*
une tarte aux pommes
apple pie

(moose) *(oh)* *(show-ko-lah)*
une mousse au chocolat
whipped chocolate pudding

(day) *(zah-nah-nah)* *(oh)* *(rome)*
des ananas au rhum
pineapple in rum

After completing **votre repas,** call **le serveur et** pay just as **vous avez** already learned in

Step 16:

Monsieur, je voudrais l'addition, s'il vous plaît.

En bas il y a une sample **carte** to help you prepare for your holiday.

RESTAURANT
RELAIS DE POSTE

LA CARTE

HORS-D'OEUVRE

Oeufs durs mayonnaise (hard-boiled eggs with mayonnaise)	16,50 F
Salade de tomates (sliced tomatoes)	16,50
Salade niçoise (mixed salad with tuna, green beans and potatoes) .	28,00
Filets d'anchois (anchovies)	28,00
Artichaut vinaigrette (artichoke with oil and vinegar sauce)......	40,50

POTAGES

Soupe à l'oignon (French onion soup)	18,00
Potage aux asperges (creamed asparagus)	19,50
Bouillabaisse (fish soup)	32,00
Bisque de homard (lobster bisque)	42,00

POISSONS ET FRUITS DE MER

Huîtres (oysters)	52,00
Coquilles Saint-Jacques (scallops)	55,00
Langoustines mayonnaise (boiled lobster with mayonnaise)	65,00
Moules (mussels)	60,00
Sole meunière (fried sole in butter)	58,50

ENTRÉES ET VIANDES

Escalope de veau à la crème (veal cutlets in cream sauce)........	70,00
Tournedos béarnaise (beef tenderloin in béarnaise sauce)........	70,00
Côtes d'agneau grillées (grilled lamb chops)....................	68,00
Daube de boeuf (marinated beef pot roast)	70,00
Canard au poivre vert (duck with green peppers)	85,00

Poulet à l'estragon (tarragon chicken)	50,00
Tripes (stomach lining of calf or beef)	55,00

LÉGUMES

Gratin dauphinois (scalloped potatoes)	18,00
Légumes de saison (seasonal vegetables)	19,00
Champignons sautés à la provençal (sautéed mushrooms).......	20,50
Salade verte (tossed green salad)	28,00

FROMAGE

Plateau de fromage, par personne (cheese selection)	35,00

DESSERTS

Pâtisserie (pastry from tray)	18,50
Glace à la fraise (strawberry ice cream)	16,50
Corbeille de fruits (choice of fruit)	16,00
Crêpes Suzette (crêpes with liqueur)	35,00
Pêche Melba (vanilla ice cream with peaches)	28,50

BOISSONS

Vin (verre)...	16,00
Vin (carafe)...	35,00
Bière	16,00
Eau minérale (mineral water)	12,50
Limonade	13,00
Jus de fruit (fruit juice)	14,00
Lait	13,00
Café	12,50
Thé	12,50

Service 15% compris

☐ **le zéphyr** *(zay-feer)* .... balmy breeze
☐ **zéro** *(zay-row)* .... zero
☐ **le zodiaque** *(zoh-dee-ak)* .... zodiac
— **Je suis des Poissons.** .... I am a "pisces."
82 ☐ **la zoologie** *(zoh-oh-loh-zhee)* .... zoology

Le petit déjeuner est un peu different *(dee-fay-rah⁽ⁿ⁾)* (little) **because it is fairly standardized et vous** will frequently take it at **votre hôtel** as **il est généralment** included in **le prix de votre chambre.** **En bas il y a** a sample of what **vous pouvez** expect to greet you **le matin.**

Petit déjeuner - Simple 26F
(sa⁽ⁿ⁾-pluh)

café au lait
coffee and steamed milk

pain

Petit déjeuner - Complet . 42F
(koh⁽ⁿ⁾-play)

café au lait

croissants

beurre et confiture
jam

Petit déjeuner à l'anglaise
in the English manner

(these additions usually only available in large hotels catering to foreigners)

jus d'orange

jus de pamplemousse
grapefruit

jambon
ham

saucisse
sausage

oeuf à la coque
egg   soft-boiled

oeuf mollet
medium-boiled

oeufs brouillés
scrambled

omelette nature

Des phrases pratiques

Combien coûte le petit déjeuner?

Je voudrais deux complets, s'il vous plaît.

Je voudrais des croissants et du thé, s'il vous plaît.

(vuh-yay) *(fare)*
Veuillez faire monter le petit déjeuner à la chambre dix,
please   have   brought up

s'il vous plaît.

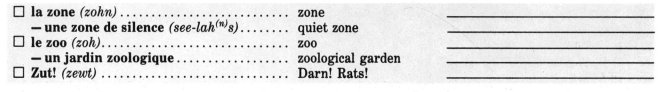

☐ **la zone** *(zohn)* . . . . zone _____
— **une zone de silence** *(see-lah⁽ⁿ⁾s)* . . . . quiet zone _____
☐ **le zoo** *(zoh)* . . . . zoo _____
— **un jardin zoologique** . . . . zoological garden _____
☐ **Zut!** *(zewt)* . . . . Darn! Rats! _____

83

Step 19

(tay-lay-phone)
Le Téléphone
telephone

(kess) *(key)*
Qu'est-ce qui est différent about **le téléphone en France?**   Well, **vous** never notice such
what

things until **vous** want to use them.   Be warned **maintenant** that **téléphones en France**

are less numerous than **en Amérique.**   Nevertheless, **le téléphone** allows you to reserve

(veel)
les chambres d'hôtel dans another **ville,** call friends, **demander des renseignements sur**
city

les billets de théâtre, de concert ou de ballet, make emergency calls, check on the hours

(mew-zay)
of a **musée,** rent **une automobile et** all those other **choses** which **nous faisons** on a daily
museum

(lee-bear-tay)
basis.   It also gives you a certain amount of **liberté quand vous pouvez** make your own

(ah-pel)
appels de téléphone.
calls

Vous pouvez trouver les téléphones in the **bureaux de poste,** on the street, in the **cafés**
to find   post offices

(zhuh-toh$^{(n)}$)
and in the lobby of **votre hôtel.**   Often **vous devez acheter** a token, called **un jeton,**

before you use a public **téléphone.**   Many public **téléphones** use plastic phone cards.   You

can buy these cards **au bureaux de poste et à la gare.**
                                        station

Voilà un téléphone public français.

So far, so good.   **Maintenant,** let's read the
instructions for using **le téléphone.**   This **est**
one of those moments when you realize,

(nuh) (swee) (pah) (zah$^{(n)}$)
Je ne suis pas en Amérique.
      am   not

So let's learn how to operate **le téléphone.**

If **vous** use **le téléphone dans un bar ou un café,** be sure to ask, "**Est-ce qu'un jeton** *(ess)* *(kuh*$^{(n)}$*)* *(zhuh-toh*$^{(n)}$*)*

(nay-say-sair)
est nécessaire?"   The **bar** employee will sell you **un jeton** to use if it is needed **et,** if not,

then **vous pouvez** use **regular pièces de monnaie.**

Consultez le tableau des taxes ci-contre et préparez votre monnaie en fonction du
indicator   of   prices   attached   prepare   depending upon

temps pendant lequel vous désirez parler, car l'appareil ne rend pas la monnaie.
time   during   which   desire   for   phone   does not return

Décrochez le combiné et composez le numéro.
lift   receiver   dial

Vous ne pourrez introduire les pièces qu'après la réponse de votre correspondant.
insert   coins   only after   party

Lorsque le demandé a répondu, la tonalité d'appel se transforme en une tonalité
when   called party   has answered   dial tone   changes   to   tone

de paiement (bip-bip-bip . . .)
payment

Introduisez immediatement les pièces.
insert

La tonalité de paiement ne s'arrête et vous ne pouvez parler que lorsque
stops   only   when

l'appareil a encaissé une somme suffisante.
has registered   sum

Pour prolonger la conversation introduisez d'autres pièces,
to   lengthen   additional

—à n'importe quel moment durant la conversation
at any time   during

—très rapidement, dès que vous reentendez la tonalité de paiement (bip-bip-bip)
quickly   as soon as   hear again

Anglais	Français	Anglais	Français
telephone	= **le téléphone**	to telephone=	**téléphoner**
		=	**faire un appel**
telephone booth	= **la cabine téléphonique**		**téléphonique**
telephone book	*(lah-new-air)* = **l'annuaire**	operator	= **le téléphoniste**
		=	**le standardiste**
telephone conversation=	**la conversation téléphonique**	token	= **le jeton**

So **maintenant vous savez comment faire un appel téléphonique en France.** **Vous** will find that **la majorité** *(ma-zhoh-ree-tay)* **des numéros en France sont huit** digits, such as **69-47-06-14.** **Il y a aussi** area codes, or **indicatifs régionaux,** *(a*$^{(n)}$*-dee-ka-teef) (ray-zhee-oh-noh)* and these are listed in **l'annuaire.** *(lah-new-air)* **Les téléphones dans les maisons** also have an added feature different from ours in that they come equipped with an extra listening device as extension phones **are** rare.

When answering **le téléphone, vous** pick up **le récepteur et** say, *(ray-sep-tur)* receiver

"**Allô?** **C'est** _____ **à l'appareil.**" *(ah)(lah-pah-ray)*
votre nom · on the phone

When saying good-bye, **vous dites,** "**À demain**" **ou** "**Au revoir.**" **Voilà** some sample *(ah) (duh-ma*$^{(n)}$*)* · until tomorrow · *(oh) (ruh-vwahr)* · good-bye

conversations au téléphone. Write them in the blanks **en bas.**
on the

Je voudrais téléphoner au Louvre. _____ *(loo-vruh)*

Je voudrais téléphoner à Chicago. *Je voudrais téléphoner à Chicago.*

Je voudrais téléphoner à Madame Le Gaul à Marseille. _____

Je voudrais téléphoner à Monsieur Le Gaul à Nice. _____

Je voudrais téléphoner à Air France à l'aéroport. _____

Je voudrais faire un appel en P. C. V. _____ *(fare)* make · *(pay-say-vay)* collect call

Où est la cabine téléphonique? _____

Où est l'annuaire? _____

Mon numéro est 53-68-70-10. _____

Quel est le numéro de votre téléphone? _____ *(kel)* what

Quel est le numéro de téléphone de l'hôtel? _____

86 **Voilà une autre conversation possible.** Listen to **les mots et comment** they are used. *(oh-truh)* another · *(poh-see-bluh)*

Thomas: Allô, c'est Monsieur Cézanne à l'appareil. Je voudrais parler à Madame Villon.

Secrétaire: Un *(a(n)-stah(n))* instant, s'il vous plaît. *(kee-tay)* Ne quittez pas. Excusez-moi, mais la
one   moment   don't hang up   but
(leen-yuh) ligne est occupée.
busy

Thomas: Répétez ça, s'il vous plaît. Je parle seulement un peu de français. *(lah(n)t-mah(n))* Parlez plus lentement.
more   slowly

Secrétaire: Excusez-moi, mais la ligne est occupée.

Thomas: Oh. Merci. *(oh)* *(ruh-vwahr)* Au revoir.

(ah(n)-kor)
Et encore une autre possibilité.
still

Christine: Je voudrais des "renseignements" pour Angoulême, s'il vous plaît.
information

Je voudrais le numéro de téléphone du Docteur Philippe Beauchamp, s'il vous plaît.

Téléphoniste: Le numéro est 72-86-45-06.

Christine: Répétez le numéro, s'il vous plaît.

Téléphoniste: Le numéro est 72-86-45-06.

Christine: Merci beaucoup. Au revoir.

Téléphoniste: À votre service. Au revoir.
you are welcome

Vous êtes maintenant ready to use any **téléphone en France.** Just take it **lentement et** speak clearly.

(noo-blee-ay) *(pah)*
N'oubliez pas that **vous pouvez** ask . . .
don't forget

Combien coûte un appel téléphonique local? _____

Combien coûte un appel téléphonique interurbain à Cannes? _____

(oh)
Combien coûte un appel téléphonique aux États-Unis? _____
United States

Combien coûte un appel téléphonique à Rome? _____

N'oubliez pas that **vous avez besoin de la monnaie ou d'un jeton pour le téléphone.**
need

Step 20

Le Métro
(may-tro)
subway

(may-tro-poh-lee-ta⁽ⁿ⁾)
Le métropolitain, commonly called **"le métro,"** est le nom pour the subway.   **Le métro à**

Paris est the quickest and cheapest form of **transport.**   It is an extensive **système** which
(trah⁽ⁿ⁾-spor) transportation   _(see-stem)_

has been expanded by an express line, **le RER** (Réseau Express Régional), going to
(air-uh-air)

(bah⁽ⁿ⁾-lee-uh)
la banlieue de Paris.   **A Paris, et dans** smaller **villes, il y a toujours l'autobus,** a slower
suburbs   of   _(veel)_ cities   _(too-zhoor)_ always

but much more scenic means of **transport.**   **Vous** may also wish to go by **taxi.**   In that
(trah⁽ⁿ⁾-spor)   _(tahx-ee)_

case, **trouvez** a **taxi** station, hail a **taxi** on the street or have one called **à votre hôtel.**
(tahx-ee)

(kel)
Quels mots sont nécessaires pour voyager en métro, en autobus ou en taxi?   Let's
what   _(nay-say-sair)_

learn them by practicing them aloud **et puis** by writing them in the blanks **en bas.**
(pwee)

(may-tro) **le métro**	_(tahx-ee)_ **le taxi**	_(kahr)_ **l'autobus/le car**

_____	_le taxi_	_____

(lah-ray)
l'arrêt = the stop _____

(leen-yuh)
la ligne = the line _____

(koh⁽ⁿ⁾-dewk-tur)
le conducteur = the driver _____

(koh⁽ⁿ⁾-troh-lur)
le contrôleur = the ticket-collector _____

Let's also review **les verbes de transport** at this point.

(moh⁽ⁿ⁾-tay)
monter = to board/to get into _____

(day-sah⁽ⁿ⁾-druh)
descendre = to get off/to go down _____ _descendre, descendre_ _____

(shah⁽ⁿ⁾-zhay)
changer (d'autobus) = to transfer _____

(vwhy-ah-zhay)
voyager = to travel _____

Maps displaying the various **lignes et arrêts sont généralement** *(leen-yuh)* *(ah-ray)* posted outside every **entrée de station** *(ah(n)-tray)* *(stah-see-oh(n))* de métro. Almost every **plan** *(plah(n))* de Paris also has a **métro** map included.

Les lignes sont color-coded to facilitate reading. **Vous achetez les tickets** on entering **la station et vous pouvez acheter un ticket ou un carnet de dix tickets.** *(kar-nay)* Check **le nom** of the last **station** on the **ligne** which you should take **et** catch **le train** traveling in that **direction.** *(dee-rek-see-oh(n))* If **vous devez changer de train,** look for **les correspondances** *(ko-ray-spoh(n)-dah(n)s)* clearly marked at each **station.** **Le système d'autobus** works similiarly. See **le plan en bas.** *(plah(n))*

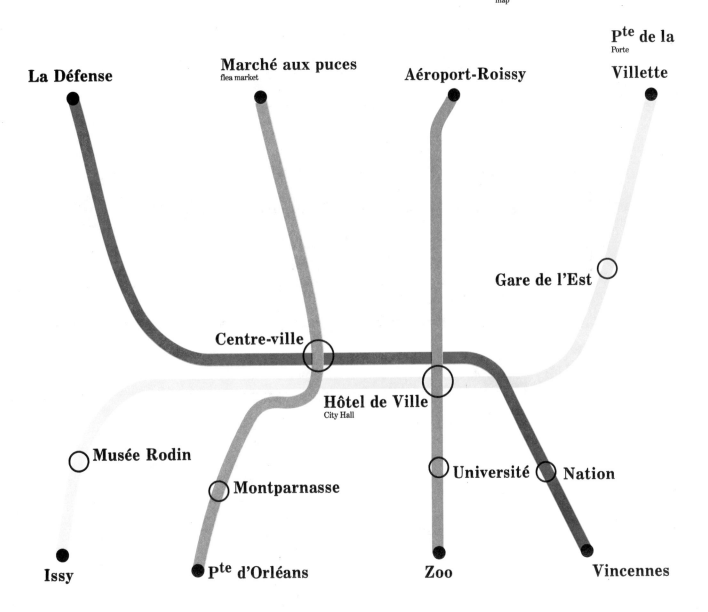

The same basic set of **mots et questions** will see you through traveling **en métro, en car, en auto ou** even **en train.**

Naturally, la (pruh-mee-air) **première** question est "où."

Où est la station de (stah-see-oh⁽ⁿ⁾) (may-tro) **métro**?

Où est l'(lah-ray) **arrêt** d'autobus?

Où est la station de taxis?

Où est la (tet) **tête** de taxis?
head

Practice the following basic **questions** out loud **et puis** write them in the blanks **à droite.**

1. Où est la station de métro? _____

   Où est l'arrêt d'autobus? *Où est l'arrêt d'autobus?*

   Où est la station de taxis? _____

2. Quelle est la (fray-kah⁽ⁿ⁾s) **fréquence** (day) **des** trains pour le Louvre? _____
   frequency

   Quelle est la fréquence des autobus pour Montparnasse? _____

   Quelle est la fréquence des taxis pour l'aéroport? _____

3. (kah⁽ⁿ⁾) **Quand** le train part-il? _____
   when

   Quand l'autobus part-il? _____

   Quand le taxi part-il? _____

4. Quand le train pour (rwah-see) **Roissy** part-il? _____

   Quand l'autobus pour Roissy part-il? _____

   Quand le taxi pour Roissy part-il? _____

5. Combien coûte un ticket de métro? _____

   Combien coûte un ticket d'autobus? _____

   Le tarif c'est combien? *Le tarif c'est combien?*

   Combien est-ce que je vous (dwah) **dois**? _____
   to you   owe

Maintenant that **vous avez** gotten into the swing of things, practice the following

patterns aloud, substituting **"autobus"** for **"métro"** et so on.

1. Où est-ce qu'on achète *(ess)* *(koh(n))* *(nah-shet)* un ticket de métro?   d'autobus?   de train?

2. Quand part le train pour La Défense?   pour le centre-ville?   pour Montparnasse?

   pour l'Hôtel de Ville?   pour l'aéroport?   pour la gare?   pour la Tour Eiffel?

3. Où est la station de métro pour aller à l'aéroport? *to go*

   Où est l'arrêt *(lah-ray)* d'autobus pour aller à la Tour *(toor)* Eiffel *(ay-fell)*?

   Où est la station de métro pour aller au *(oh)* centre-ville *(sah(n)-truh-veel)*?

   Où est l'arrêt d'autobus pour aller au Zoo *(zoh)*?

   Où est la station de métro pour aller au Musée *(mew-zay)* Rodin *(ro-da(n))*?

   Où est l'arrêt d'autobus pour aller à la Gare de l'Est *(lest)*?

   Où est la station de métro pour aller à l'université?

   Où est l'arrêt d'autobus pour aller au marché aux puces?

Lisez la conversation suivante, très typique *(tee-peek)*, et écrivez- la *(ay-kree-vay)* *(lah)* in the blanks à droite. *it*

Quelle *(kel)* ligne va *(vah)* à Vincennes *(va(n)-sen)*? _____
which   *goes*

La ligne rouge va à Vincennes? _____

A quelle fréquence? _____

Toutes *(toot)* les dix minutes. _____ *Toutes les dix minutes.* _____
every

Dois-je *(dwah-zh)* changer de train? _____
must *I*

Oui, au centre-ville.   Vous avez une correspondance *(ko-ray-spoh(n)-dah(n)s)* **à la station "Opéra."**
connection

Oui, au centre-ville. _____

Il *(eel)* **faut** *(foh)* **combien de temps d'ici à Vincennes?** _____
it is necessary   *from here*

Il *(eel)* **faut** *(foh)* **20 minutes.** _____

Combien coûte le ticket pour Vincennes? _____

Un franc cinquante. _____

Pouvez-vous translate the following thoughts **en français?** **Les réponses sont en bas.**

1. Where is the subway stop? _____

2. What costs a ticket to City Hall? _____

3. How often do the buses go to the airport? _____

4. Where does one buy a subway ticket? _____

5. Where is the bus stop? _____ *Où est l'arrêt d'autobus?*

6. I would like to get out. _____

7. Must I transfer? _____

8. Where must I transfer? _____

Voilà encore trois verbes.

(lah-vay)
laver = to wash

(pear-druh)
perdre = to lose

(eel)(foh)
il faut = it is necessary

laver, laver _____ _____

You know the basic "plug-in" formula, so translate the following thoughts **avec ces nouveaux verbes.** **Les réponses sont aussi en bas.**

1. I wash the jacket. _____

2. You lose the book. _____

3. It takes (is necessary) 20 minutes to go to Vincennes. _____

4. It takes three hours by car. _____

(vah⁽ⁿ⁾t)   *(lah-shah)*

La Vente et l'Achat

selling   buying

Shopping abroad **est** exciting. The simple everyday task of buying **un litre de lait ou**

(pohm)
une **pomme** becomes a challenge that **vous** should **maintenant** be able to meet quickly **et**
apple

(soo-vuh-neer)
easily. Of course, **vous** will purchase **des souvenirs, des timbres-poste et des cartes**
souvenirs

(ah-spee-reen)
postales, but **n'oubliez pas** those many other **choses** ranging from shoelaces to **aspirine**
aspirin

(lee-brair-ree)
that **vous** might need unexpectedly. **Savez-vous la différence entre une librairie et une**
know   bookstore

(boo-shuh-ree)   *(boo-teek)*   *(ma-gah-za⁽ⁿ⁾)*
boucherie? **Non.** Let's learn about the different **boutiques et magasins en France.**
butcher shop   shops   stores

(plah⁽ⁿ⁾)   *(sek-see-oh⁽ⁿ⁾)*
En bas il y a un plan d'une section de Paris.
map

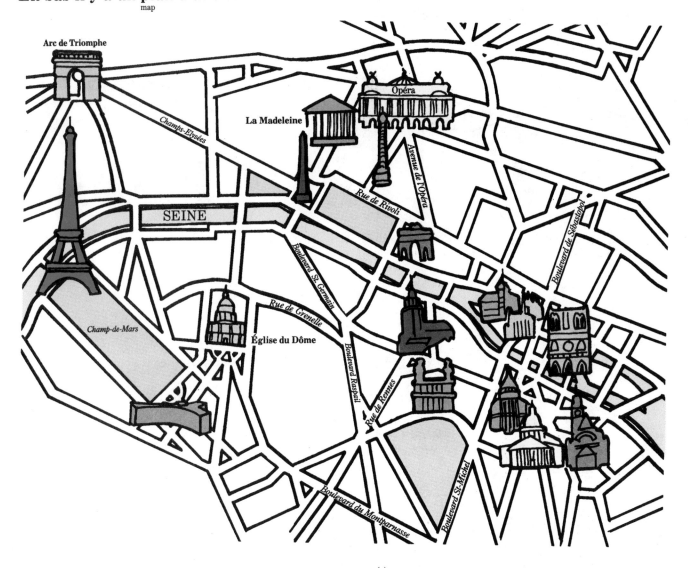

(ma-gah-za⁽ⁿ⁾)
Sur les pages suivantes il y a all types of **magasins en France.** Be sure to fill in the

blanks **sous les images avec le nom du magasin.**

(boo-lah(n)-zhuh-ree)
la boulangerie,
bakery
(oh(n)) (nah-shet)
où on achète le pain

(boo-shuh-ree)
la boucherie,
butcher shop
(vee-ah(n)nd)
où on achète la viande
meat

(blah(n)-shee-suh-ree)
la blanchisserie,
laundry
(vet-mah(n))
où on lave les vêtements
washes   clothes

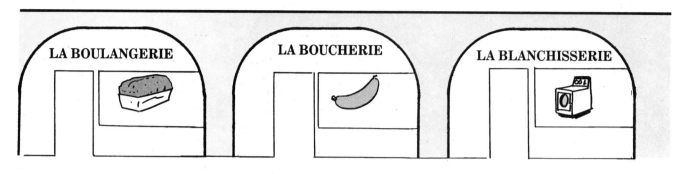

LA BOULANGERIE   LA BOUCHERIE   LA BLANCHISSERIE

le café,

(bwah)
où on boit le café

(ka(n)-ky-yuh-ree)
la quincaillerie,
hardware store
(peel)
où on achète la pile
battery

(far-mah-see)
la pharmacie,
(lah-spee-reen)
où on achète l'aspirine

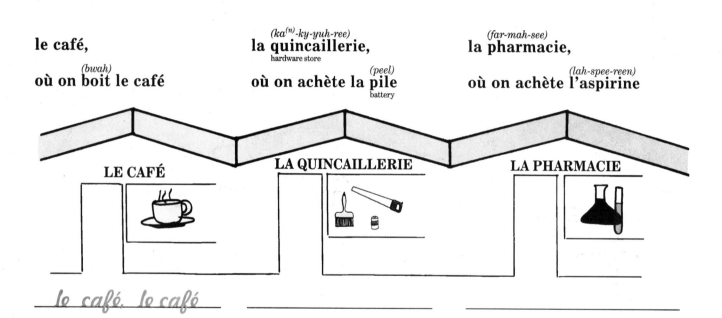

LE CAFÉ   LA QUINCAILLERIE   LA PHARMACIE

le café, le café

(flur-east)
le fleuriste,
florist

où on achète les fleurs

(tah-bah)
le bureau de tabac,
tobacco store

où on achète le tabac
tobacco
(see-gah-ret)
et les cigarettes

(koh(n)-fee-suh-ree)
la confiserie,
confectionary
(boh(n)-boh(n))
où on achète les bonbons
(show-ko-lah)
et le chocolat

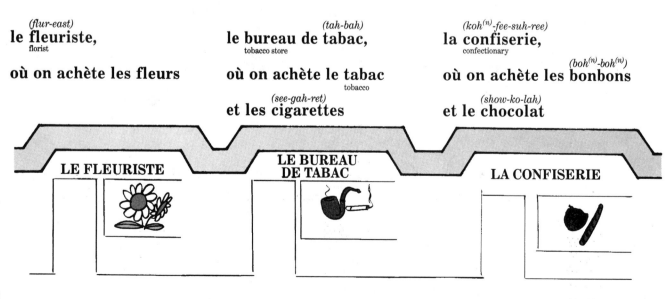

LE FLEURISTE   LE BUREAU DE TABAC   LA CONFISERIE

(lay-tuh-ree) (kray-muh-ree)
la laiterie/la crémerie,

où on achète le lait

(pah-tee-suh-ree)
la pâtisserie,
pastry shop

où on achète les pâtisseries
pastries

(mar-shah⁽ⁿ⁾) (lay-gewm)
le marchand de légumes,
seller   vegetables

où on achète les légumes

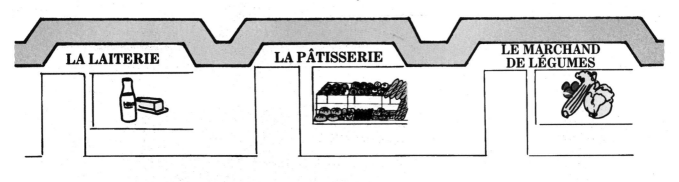

LA LAITERIE   LA PÂTISSERIE   LE MARCHAND DE LÉGUMES

(par-keeng)
le parking
parking lot

(gar)
où on gare l'auto
park

(kwah-fur)
le coiffeur,
hairdresser

(koop) (shuh-vuh)
où on coupe les cheveux
cuts   hair

(tie-yur)
le tailleur,
tailor

(vet-mah⁽ⁿ⁾)
où on fait les vêtements
makes

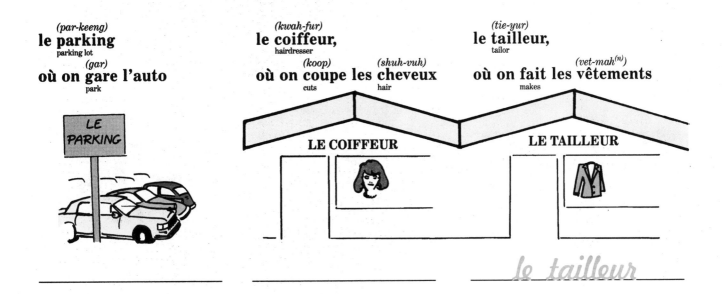

LE PARKING   LE COIFFEUR   LE TAILLEUR

le tailleur

le bureau de poste,
post office

où on achète les timbres

(ko-mee-sah-ree-ah)
le commissariat de police,
police station

(poh-lease)
où on trouve la police

la banque,

(shah⁽ⁿ⁾zh)
où on change l'argent et
exchanges

(toosh) (shek)
touche le chèque
cashes

LE BUREAU DE POSTE   LE COMMISSARIAT DE POLICE   LA BANQUE

(lay-pee-suh-ree)
l'épicerie,
grocery store

où on achète la viande,

les fruits et le lait

(shar-kew-tuh-ree)
la charcuterie,
delicatessen

(soh-see-soh⁽ⁿ⁾)
où on achète le saucisson
salami/sausage

(soh-sees)
et la saucisse

(fwee-tee-ay)
le fruitier,
fruit vendor

où on achète les fruits

L'ÉPICERIE

LA CHARCUTERIE

LE FRUITIER

(see-nay-mah)
le cinéma,

(vwah)
où on voit le film
sees

(kee-osk)
le kiosque,
newstand

où on achète les

(zhoor-no)
journaux et les revues

(neh-twhy-yahzh) *(sek)*
le nettoyage à sec,
dry cleaning

où on lave les

(shee-meek-mah⁽ⁿ⁾)
vêtements chimiquement
chemically

LE CINÉMA

LE KIOSQUE

LE NETTOYAGE À SEC

le cinéma

(pah-peh-tuh-ree)
la papeterie,
stationery store

où on achète le papier,

le stylo et le crayon

(lee-brair-ree)
la librairie,
bookstore

où on achète et

(vah⁽ⁿ⁾)
vend les livres
sells

(grah⁽ⁿ⁾) *(ma-gah-za⁽ⁿ⁾)*
le grand magasin,
department store

(too)
où on achète tout
everything

(see Step 22)

LA PAPETERIE

LA LIBRAIRIE

LE GRAND MAGASIN

(mar-shay)
le marché, où on
market

achète les légumes et fruits

(sue-pear-mar-shay)
le supermarché,

où on achète tout
everything

(stah-see-oh(n))(day-sah(n))
la station d'essence,
gas station

où on achète l'essence

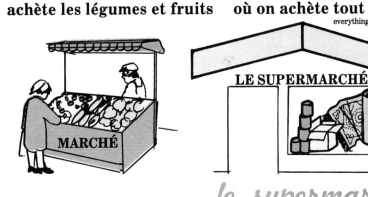

le supermarché

(lah-zhah(n)s) (vwhy-ahzh)
l'agence de voyage,
travel agency

où on achète les

billets d'avion

(lor-low-zhuh-ree)
l'horlogerie
clock and watchmaker's shop

où on achète les horloges

(pwah-soh(n)-nuh-ree)
la poissonnerie
fish market

(pwah-soh(n))
où on achète le poisson
fish

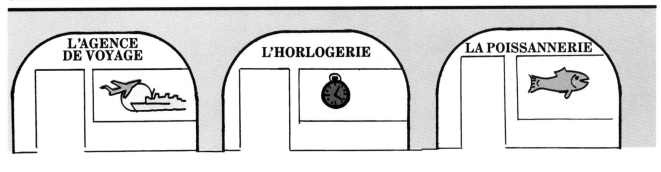

Quand les magasins français sont-ils ouverts? **(oo-vair)** **Les magasins français sont**
are they open

généralement ouverts de lundi à samedi, de 9:00 à 18:30. **Beaucoup de petits**

magasins will close over the lunch hour **(12:00 — 14:00),** although this is increasingly less

true **à Paris.** Some foodshops **sont ouverts le dimanche, et** it is often a family ritual to
on Sundays

make a trip **à la boulangerie ou à la pâtisserie** to pick up **le pain et** special weekend

(gah-toe) **(toh-see)**
gâteau. Many shops **sont aussi** closed **le lundi.** Local, open-air **marchés sont** truly **une**
cake also

(ek-spay-ree-ah(n)s) **(lay) (zuhr)**
expérience, so be sure to check **les heures** of the one closest to **votre hôtel.**

(ee) (ah-teel)
Y a-t-il anything else which makes **les magasins français différents** from **les magasins**
is there

américains? Oui. Look at **les images à la prochaine page.** 97

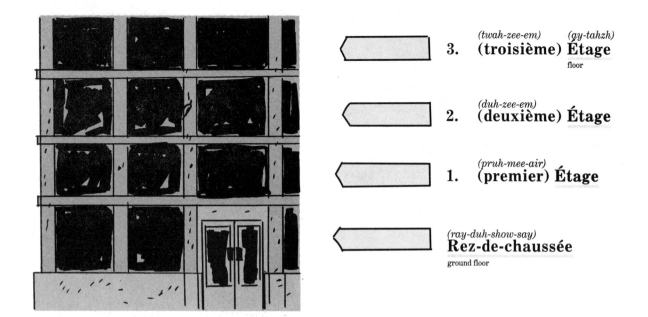

(ray-duh-show-say)

En France the ground floor **s'appelle "le rez-de-chaussée."** The first floor **est** the next floor up **et** so on. Now that **vous** know **les noms pour les magasins français,** let's practice shopping.

I. First step — Où?

<u>**Où est la laiterie?**</u>　　　　<u>**Où est la banque?**</u>　　　　<u>**Où est le cinéma?**</u>

Go through **les magasins** introduced in this Step **et** ask , **"Où"** avec **chaque** magasin.
(shahk)
each

Another way of asking **où** is to ask

(ee)(ah-teel) *(pray)* *(dee-see)*
Y a-t-il une laiterie près d'ici?　　　　　　**Y a-t-il une banque près d'ici?**
near here

Go through **les magasins** again using **cette nouvelle question.**
this

II. Next step — tell them what **vous** are looking for, need **ou voudriez!**

1) **J'ai besoin de . . .**　*J'ai besoin de* _____

2) **Avez vous . . . ?**　_____

3) **Je voudrais . . .**　_____

J'ai besoin d'un crayon.

Avez-vous un crayon?

Je voudrais un crayon.

J'ai besoin d'un kilo de pommes. *(pohm)*

Avez-vous un kilo de pommes?

Je voudrais un kilo de pommes.

Go through the glossary at the end of this **ce livre et** select **vingt mots.** Drill the above patterns **avec ces vingt mots.** Don't cheat. Drill them **aujourd'hui. Maintenant,** take **encore vingt mots de votre** glossary **et** do the same.

more

III. Next step — find out **combien ça coûte.**

1) **Combien est-ce?** *(ess)* _____

2) **Combien est-ce que ça coûte?** *(kuh) (sah)* _____

Combien coûte le crayon? *(koot)*

Combien coûte la carte-postale? *(koot)*

Combien coûte le timbre?

Combien coûte un kilo de pommes?

Combien coûte un kilo d'oranges?

Combien coûte un kilo de viande?

Using the same **mots** that **vous** selected **en haut,** drill **ces questions aussi.**

IV. If **vous ne savez pas où trouver** something, **vous demandez** *(duh-mah⁽ⁿ⁾-day)*
ask

Où est-ce qu'on achète de l'aspirine? *(lah-spee-reen)*

Où est-ce qu'on achète des lunettes de soleil? *(lew-net) (so-lay)*

Once **vous trouvez** what **vous** would like, **vous dites,**

Je voudrais ça, s'il vous plaît.

Ou, if **vous** would not like it,

Je ne voudrais pas ça, merci.

Vous êtes maintenant all set to shop for anything!

Le Grand Magasin
(grah$^{(n)}$)   (ma-gah-zah$^{(n)}$)
department store

At this point, **vous** should just about be ready for **votre voyage en France.** **Vous** have

gone shopping for those last-minute odds 'n ends.   Most likely, the store directory at your

local **grand magasin** did not look like the one **en bas.**   **Vous** know already **beaucoup de**

mots et vous pouvez guess at **beaucoup d'autres.** (doh-truh) others   **Vous savez qu'** "**enfant**" **est français**
know   that

pour "child", so if **vous avez besoin de** something **pour un enfant, vous** would probably

look on the **deuxième ou troisième étage, n'est-ce pas?** (duh-zee-em) (twah-zee-em) (ay-tahzh)

6.ME ÉTAGE	boulangerie cafétéria charcuterie alcool	volaille alimentation fruits légumes	produits congelés vin gibier viande
5.ME ÉTAGE	lits linge miroirs	ameublement lampes tapis	tableaux électroménager
4.ME ÉTAGE	vaisselle cristal	service de table ameublement de cuisine	clés faïence porcelaine
3.ME ÉTAGE	livres télévisions meubles d'enfant jouets	radios instruments de musique papeterie disques	tabac restaurant journaux revues
2.ME ÉTAGE	tout pour l'enfant vêtements de femme chapeaux de femme	vetements d'homme chaussures d'enfant photo	toilettes antiquités
1.ER ÉTAGE	accessoires d'auto lingerie mouchoirs	maillots de bain chaussures de femmes chaussures d'homme	équipement de sport outils mobilier de camping
R	parapluies cartes chapeaux d'homme bijouterie	gants maroquinerie chaussettes ceintures	pendules/montres parfumerie confiserie

Let's start a check **liste pour votre voyage.** (least)   Besides **vetements, de quoi avez-vous**
(vet-mah$^{(n)}$) (kwah)
what

besoin? Qu'est-ce qu'il faut en Europe? (kess) (keel)
what   is necessary

(pass-por)
le passeport

(bee-yay)
le billet

(vah-leez)
la valise

_____ ☐

_____ ☐

la valise ☑

(sahk) (ah) (ma^{(n)})
le sac à main

(port-fuh-yuh)
le portefeuille

(lar-zhah^{(n)})
l'argent

_____ ☐

_____ ☐

_____ ☐

(lah-pah-ray)
l'appareil-photo

(peh-lee-kewl)
la pellicule

_____ ☐

_____ ☐

(pruh-nay)
Prenez les huit labels **suivantes et** label **ces choses aujourd'hui.** Better yet, assemble
take

them **dans un coin de votre maison.**
of

Voyagez-vous en France en été ou en hiver? **N'oubliez pas . . .**
don't forget

(my-oh) *(ba^{(n)})*
les maillots de bain

(sah^{(n)}-dahl)
les sandales

_____ ☐

_____ ☐

(noh^{(n)}) (plew)
N'oubliez pas non plus the basic toiletries!
either

(sah-voh^{(n)})
le savon

(brohs) (ah) (dah^{(n)})
la brosse à dents

(dah^{(n)}-tee-frees)
le dentifrice

(rah-zwahr)
le rasoir

(day-oh-doh-rah^{(n)})
le déodorant

(pen-yuh)
le peigne

le savon ☑

_____ ☐

_____ ☐

_____ ☐

_____ ☐

_____ ☐ **101**

For the rest of the **choses,** let's start **avec** the outside layers **et** work our way in.

(mah⁽ⁿ⁾-toe)
le manteau _____ ☐

(lah⁽ⁿ⁾-pear-may-ah-bluh)
l'imperméable _____ ☐

(pah-rah-plew-ee)
le parapluie _____ ☐

(gah⁽ⁿ⁾)
les gants _____ ☐

(shah-poh)
le chapeau _____ ☐

(boat)
la botte _____ ☐

(show-sewr)
la chaussure *la chaussure* ☑

(show-set)
la chaussette _____ ☐

(bah)
les bas _____ ☐

(pruh-nay)
Prenez les quinze labels **suivantes et** label **ces choses.** Check **et** make sure that **elles**
take

(proh-pruh) *(rehst)*
sont propres et ready **pour votre voyage.** Be sure to do the same **avec le reste des**
clean rest of the

choses that **vous** pack. Check them off on **cette liste** as **vous** organize them. From **now**

on, **vous avez du "dentifrice" et non pas** "toothpaste."
not

(pee-zhah-mah)
le pyjama *le pyjama* ☑

(shuh-meez) *(nwee)*
la chemise de nuit _____ ☐

(rohb) *(shah⁽ⁿ⁾-bruh)*
la robe de chambre _____ ☐

(pah⁽ⁿ⁾-too-fluh)
les pantoufles _____ ☐

(puhv) *(plahzh)*
102 **La robe de chambre et les pantoufles peuvent aussi** double **pour vous à la plage!**
can beach

(koh(n)-play)
le complet _____ ☐

(krah-vaht)
la cravate _____ ☐

(moo-shwahr)
le mouchoir _____ ☐

(shuh-meez)
la chemise _____ ☐

(veh-stoh(n))
le veston _____ ☐

(pah(n)-tah-loh(n))
le pantalon _____ ☐

(rohb)
la robe _____ ☐

(blooz)
la blouse _____ ☐

(zhewp)
la jupe _la jupe, la jupe_ ☑

(shah(n)-dye)
le chandail _____ ☐

(soo-tee-a(n)-gorzh)
le soutien-gorge _____ ☐

(koh(n)-bee-nay-zoh(n))
la combinaison _____ ☐

(sleep)
les slips _____ ☐

(tree-ko) (poh)
le tricot de peau _____ ☐

Having assembled **ces choses, vous êtes préparé pour votre voyage.** However, being
(pray-pah-ray) / prepared

human means occasionally forgetting something. Look again at **le grand maison**

directory.

À quel étage trouvez-vous . . .
on   which

vêtements d'homme?   Au ____2.me____ étage.

un chapeau pour une dame?   Au _____ étage.

livres?   Au _____ étage.

lingerie?   Au _____ étage.

103

cristal?   Au ＿＿＿＿＿＿＿＿＿＿ étage.

parfum?   Au ＿＿＿＿＿＿＿＿＿＿ .

vêtements de femme?   Au ＿＿＿＿＿＿＿＿＿＿ étage.

Maintenant, just remember your basic **questions.** **Répétez la conversation typique** *(tee-peek)* **en bas** out loud **et puis** by filling in the blanks.

Où est-ce qu'on trouve les pantalons de femme? *Où* ＿＿＿＿＿＿＿＿＿＿＿＿＿＿

Dans le rayon *(ray-oh[n])* **de vêtements de femme.** *Dans* ＿＿＿＿＿＿＿＿＿＿＿＿
              department

Où est le rayon de vêtements de femme? *Où* ＿＿＿＿＿＿＿＿＿＿＿＿＿＿＿

Au deuxième étage. ＿＿＿＿＿＿＿＿＿＿＿＿＿＿＿＿＿＿＿＿

Où est-ce qu'on trouve le savon et le dentifrice? ＿＿＿＿＿＿＿＿＿＿＿＿

Au rez-de-chaussée. ＿＿＿＿＿＿＿＿＿＿＿＿＿＿＿＿＿＿＿

Aussi, n'oubliez pas de demander *(duh-mah[n]-day)* **. . .**
                    ask

Où est l'ascenseur? *(lah-sah[n]-sur)* *Où* ＿＿＿＿＿＿＿＿＿＿＿＿
         elevator

Où est l'escalier? *(leh-skah-lee-ay)* *Où* ＿＿＿＿＿＿＿＿＿＿＿＿
        steps

Où est l'escalier roulant? *(leh-skah-lee-ay) (roo-lah[n])* ＿＿＿＿＿＿＿＿＿＿
      escalator

Whether **vous avez besoin d'un pantalon de femme ou d'une chemise d'homme, les mots nécessaires sont** the same. Just practice, practice, practice.

104

Quelle taille? *(tie)* size

_____

Quelle pointure? *(pwa(n)-tewr)* size for shoes and gloves

_____

Ça me va. *(muh) (vah)* me fits

Ça me va.

Ça ne me va pas. *(nuh) (muh) (vah) (pah)* doesn't fit

_____

Je prends ça. *(prah(n)) (sah)* take that

_____

Combien est-ce?

_____

C'est tout, merci beaucoup. that's all

_____

Clothing Sizes: **FEMMES**

chaussures									
American	5	5½	6	6½	7	7½	8	8½	9
Continental	35	35	36	37	38	38	38	39	40

vêtements					
American	8	10	12	14	16	18
Continental	36	38	40	42	44	46

blouses, chandails						
American	32	34	36	38	40	42	44
Continental	40	42	44	46	48	50	52

Clothing Sizes: **HOMMES**

chaussures									
American	7	7½	8	8½	9	9½	10	10½	11	11½
Continental	39	40	41	42	43	43	44	44	45	45

vêtements							
American	34	36	38	40	42	44	46	48
Continental	44	46	48	50	52	54	56	58

chemises							
American	14	14½	15	15½	16	16½	17	17½
Continental	36	37	38	39	40	41	42	43

Maintenant, vous êtes préparé pour votre voyage. *(pray-pah-ray)* **Vous savez tout** that you need.

The next Step will give you a quick review of international road signs **et** then **vous** are

off to **l'aéroport.** **Bon voyage! Amusez-vous bien!**

Step 23

 = **Dangerous Intersection**

Voilà some of the most important **signalisations** *(seen-yahl-ee-zah-see-oh(n))* [signs] **routières** *(roo-tee-air)* [road] **internationales.** *(a(n)-tair-nah-see-oh(n)-nahl)* [international] Remember that **en France** a basic rule of the road is **priorité** *(pree-oh-ree-tay)* [yield] **à droite.** *(koh(n)-dwee-zay)* [to the right] **Conduisez** *(koh(n)-dwee-zay)* [drive] **prudemment!** *(prew-duh-mah(n))* [carefully] **Bon voyage!**

Danger

Dangerous curve

Dangerous intersection

Closed to all vehicles

Prohibited for motor vehicles

Prohibited for motor vehicles on Sundays and holidays

No entry

Stop

Main road ahead, yield the right of way

You have the right of way

Additional sign indicating the right of way

One-way street

Dead-end street

Detour

Traffic circle

No left turn

No U-turn

No parking

No parking or waiting

No passing

Speed limit

End of speed limit

Beginning of **autoroute**

Railroad crossing
240 meters

Railroad crossing
160 meters

Railroad crossing
80 meters

Customs

Federal Highway
Number

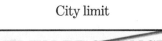

End of city limit

Parking permitted

Roads ends, water
ahead

GLOSSARY

A

a/avoir .... has/to have
à .... at, to, in
  à côté de .... next to
  à demain .... till tomorrow
  à droite .... to the right
  à gauche .... to the left
accident, le .... accident
acheter .... to buy
addition, la .... bill in a restaurant
adresse, la .... address
aéroport, le .... airport
Afrique, la .... Africa
Afrique du sud, la .... South Africa
agence de location des voitures, la .... car rental agency
agence de voyage, la .... travel agency
ai/avoir .... have/to have
aidez-moi .... help me! aid me!
AJ, la .... youth hostel
alcool, le .... alcohol
Allemagne, la .... Germany
aller .... to go, one way
aller et retour .... round trip
américain (e) .... American
Amérique, la .... America
ameublement, le .... furnishings
amusez-vous .... amuse yourself
an, le .... year
ananas, le .... pineapple
anglais (e) .... English
Angleterre, la .... England
animal, le .... animal
année, la .... year
annuaire, le .... telephone book
août, le .... August
appareil, le .... gadget, appliance
appartement, le .... apartment
s'appeler .... to be called
appel téléphonique, le .... telephone call
appétit, le .... appetite
apprendre .... to learn
approximativement .... approximately
après-midi, le .... afternoon
arbre, le .... tree
argent, le .... money
armoire, la .... closet, wardrobe
arrêt, le .... stop, arrest
arrivée, la .... arrival
arriver .... to arrive
ascenseur, le .... elevator
assiette, la .... plate
assis (e) .... seated
attendre .... to wait for
atterrir .... to land
au .... in the, at the
auberge, la .... country inn
auberge de la jeunesse, la .... youth hostel
au coin .... on the corner
au milieu .... in the middle
au revoir .... goodbye
au-dessus de .... over
aujourd'hui .... today
aussi .... also
auto, la .... car
autobus, le .... bus
automobile à louer, la .... rental car
automne, le .... Autumn
autoroute, la .... freeway
autre .... another
avec .... with
avez/avoir .... have/to have
avion, le .... airplane
avoir .... to have
avoir besoin de .... to need
avons/avoir .... have/to have
avril .... April

B

baigner .... to bathe
balcon, le .... balcony
balle, la .... ball
banane, la .... banana
banc, le .... bench
banlieue, la .... suburbs
banque, la .... bank
bas .... low
  en bas .... below, downstairs
basé .... based
bateau, le .... boat
beau .... beautiful
beaucoup .... many, a lot
belle .... beautiful
beurre, le .... butter
bicyclette, la .... bicycle
bien .... well
  pas bien .... not too well
bien sûr .... of course
bière, la .... beer
bijouterie, la .... jewelry
billet, le .... airplane/train ticket
billet de banque, le .... banknote
bistro, le .... restaurant
blanc, blanche .... white
blanchisserie, la .... laundry
bleu (e) .... blue
blouse, la .... blouse
boeuf, le .... beef
boire .... to drink
bois, les .... woods
boisson, la .... beverage
boîte aux lettres, la .... mailbox
bon/bonne .... good
bon appétit .... enjoy your meal
bonbon, le .... candy
bonjour .... good morning, good afternoon
bonne chance .... good luck
bonne nuit .... good night
bonsoir .... good evening
botte, la .... boot
boucherie, la .... butcher's shop
boulangerie, la .... bakery
bouteille, la .... bottle
boutique, la .... shop
brasserie, la .... beer-saloon, restaurant
bref .... brief, short
brosse à dents, la .... toothbrush
brouillard, le .... fog
bureau, le .... desk, office
bureau de change, le .... money-exchange counter

C

ça .... that, it
cabine téléphonique, la .... telephone booth
cabinets, les .... toilets
café, le .... cafe
café au lait .... coffee and steamed milk
caisse, la .... cashier, register
calendrier, le .... calender
canapé, le .... sofa
car .... because, for
car, le .... bus
carte, la .... menu, map
carte postale, la .... postcard
cathédrale, la .... cathedral
catholique .... Catholic
ce, cette .... that, this
ceinture, la .... belt
cendrier, le .... ashtray
cent .... one hundred
centime, le .... centime
centre, le .... center
cerise, la .... cherry
ces .... these, those
c'est .... it is
chaise, la .... chair
chambre, la .... room
chambre à coucher, la .... bedroom
chandail, le .... sweater
changement, le .... change
changer (de train, d'autobus) .... to transfer, exchange (money)
chapeau, le .... hat
charcuterie, la .... delicatessen
chat, le .... cat
château, le .... castle
chaud (e) .... hot
chaussette, la .... sock
chaussure, la .... shoe
chef, le .... cook
chemise, la .... shirt
  chemise de nuit, la .... nightshirt
chèque, le .... bank check
cher, chère .... expensive
cheveux, les .... hair
chien, le .... dog
cinquante .... fifty
clé, la .... key
coiffeur, le .... hairdresser
coin, le .... corner
colis, le .... package
combien .... how much
combinaison, la .... slip (undergarment)
commander .... to order
commencer .... to begin
comment .... how
commissariat de police, le .... police station
compagnie, la .... company
compartiment, le .... compartment
complet, le .... suit (clothes)
composer .... to compose, dial (a telephone)
comprendre .... to understand
compris .... included
concierge, le/la .... hall-porter
conducteur, le .... driver
conduire .... to drive
confiserie, la .... confectionery
confiture, la .... jam
continuer .... to continue
contravention, la .... parking ticket
contrôleur, le .... ticket collector
corbeille à papier, la .... wastebasket
correspondences, les .... connections
côté, le .... side
  à côté de .... beside, near, next to
couchette, la .... berth
couleur, la .... color
couloir, le .... hallway
couper .... to cut
courrier, le .... mail
court (e) .... short
cousin, le .... cousin (male)
cousine, la .... cousin (female)
coûte/coûter .... costs/to cost
couteau, le .... knife
coutume, la .... custom, habit
couverture, la .... blanket
cravate, la .... necktie
crayon, le .... pencil
crémerie, la .... dairy
cristal, le .... crystal
croissant, le .... crescent roll
cueillir .... to pick
cuiller, la .... spoon
cuisine, la .... kitchen
cuisinière, la .... stove
cuit (e) .... cooked
  cuit au four .... baked

D

dame, la .... lady
dans .... in
danse, la .... dance

de . . . . of, from
de, de l', de la, des, du . . . . some
décembre, le . . . . December
déclaration, la . . . . declaration
défense d'entrer . . . . do not enter
degré, le . . . . degree
déjà . . . . already
déjà vu . . . . already seen
délicieux, délicieuse . . . . delicious
demain . . . . tomorrow
à demain . . . . till tomorrow
demander . . . . to ask, ask for
demi (e) . . . . half
départ, le . . . . departure
derrière . . . . behind
désir, le . . . . desire
deux . . . . two
devant . . . . in front of
d'ici . . . . from here
dictionnaire, le . . . . dictionary
difficile . . . . difficult
dimanche, le . . . . Sunday
dire . . . . to say
dit/dire . . . . says/to say
dix . . . . ten
dix-huit . . . . eighteen
dix-neuf . . . . nineteen
dix-sept . . . . seventeen
docteur, le . . . . doctor
donc . . . . therefore, so
dormir . . . . to sleep
douce . . . . fresh (water), sweet, soft
doucement . . . . softly, gently
douche, la . . . . shower
douze . . . . twelve
drap de bain, le . . . . bath sheet

<table>
<tr><td>E</td></tr>
</table>

eau, la . . . . water
école, la . . . . school
écrire . . . . to write
église, la . . . . church
elle . . . . it, she
elles . . . . they
en . . . . in
encore . . . . again, still
enfants, les . . . . children
entre . . . . between
entrée, la . . . . entry
entrée interdite . . . . do not enter
entrée latérale . . . . side entry
entrée principale . . . . main entry
entrées, les . . . . main dishes
entrer . . . . to go in, enter
envoyer . . . . to send
escalier, le . . . . stairs
escalier roulant, le . . . . escalator
Espagne, la . . . . Spain
essence, la . . . . gasoline
est, le . . . . east
est/être . . . . is/to be
est-ce . . . . is it
et . . . . and
étage, le . . . . floor, story
état, le . . . . state
États-Unis d'Amérique . . . . USA
était . . . . was
été, le . . . . summer
êtes/être . . . . are/to be
étranger, étrangère . . . . foreign
Europe, la . . . . Europe
européen, européenne . . . . European
excusez-moi . . . . excuse me
exemple, le . . . . example
extrêmement . . . . extremely

<table>
<tr><td>F</td></tr>
</table>

F . . . . abbrev. for franc
facile . . . . easy

faim, la . . . . hunger
faire . . . . to do, make
faire un appel téléphonique . to telephone
famille, la . . . . family
farci (e) . . . . stuffed
femme, la . . . . woman
fenêtre, la . . . . window
fermé (e) . . . . closed
fête, la . . . . feast, festival
feuille, la . . . . sheet of paper
février, le . . . . February
fille, la . . . . girl, daughter
fils, le . . . . son
fin, la . . . . end
fleur, la . . . . flower
fleuriste, le . . . . florist
foi, la . . . . faith
football, le . . . . soccer
forêt, la . . . . forest
forme, la . . . . form, shape
formuler . . . . to formulate
fort (e) . . . . strong, loudly
foyer, le . . . . home, hearth, lobby
frais . . . . fresh, cool
franc, le . . . . franc
français (e) . . . . French
Français, les . . . . the French people
France, la . . . . France
fréquence, la . . . . frequency
frère, le . . . . brother
frit (e) . . . . fried
froid (e) . . . . cold
fruit, le . . . . fruit
fumer . . . . to smoke

<table>
<tr><td>G</td></tr>
</table>

gant de toilette, le . . . . wash glove
garage, le . . . . garage
garçon, le . . . . boy, waiter
gare, la . . . . train station
gâteau, le . . . . cake
gauche . . . . left
à gauche . . . . to the left
généralement . . . . generally
gibier, le . . . . wild game
glace, la . . . . mirror, ice, ice cream
gouvernement, le . . . . government
grand (e) . . . . large, tall
grand-mère, la . . . . grandmother
grand-père, le . . . . grandfather
grande serviette, la . . . . large towel
grands-parents, les . . . . grandparents
grillé (e) . . . . grilled
gris (e) . . . . gray
gros, grosse . . . . thick, big
guichet, le . . . . counter, window

<table>
<tr><td>H</td></tr>
</table>

habiter . . . . to live, reside
haut (e) . . . . high
en haut . . . . above
heure, la . . . . hour
hier . . . . yesterday
hiver, le . . . . winter
homme, le . . . . man
horaire, le . . . . timetable
horloge, la . . . . large clock
horlogerie, la . . . .
. . . . clock and watchmaker's shop
hors-d'oeuvre, le . . . . appetizer
hôtel, le . . . . hotel
hôtelier, le . . . . hotelkeeper
huit . . . . eight

<table>
<tr><td>I</td></tr>
</table>

ici . . . . here
idée, la . . . . idea
identique . . . . identical
il . . . . it, he

île, la . . . . island
il faut . . . . it is necessary
il n'y a pas de quoi . . . .
. . . . you're welcome, it's nothing
ils . . . . they
image, la . . . . picture
imperméable, le . . . . raincoat
important (e) . . . . important
indicatif régional, le . . . . area code
industrie, la . . . . industry
ingénieur, le . . . . engineer
institut, le . . . . institute
interdit (e) . . . . prohibited
intéressant (e) . . . . interesting
intérêt, le . . . . interest
intérieur, le . . . . inside, interior
à l'intérieur . . . . within
introduire . . . . to introduce, insert
Irlande, la . . . . Ireland
Italie, la . . . . Italy
italien, italienne . . . . Italian

<table>
<tr><td>J</td></tr>
</table>

jambon, le . . . . ham
janvier, le . . . . January
Japon, le . . . . Japan
japonais (e) . . . . Japanese
jaquette, la . . . . woman's jacket
jardin, le . . . . garden
jaune . . . . yellow
je I
jeton, le . . . . token for telephone calls
jeudi, le . . . . Thursday
jeunesse, la . . . . . . young people, youth
jouet, le . . . . toy
jour, le . . . . day
journal, le . . . . newspaper
juif, juive . . . . Jewish
juillet, le . . . . July
juin, le . . . . June
jupe, la . . . . skirt
jus, le . . . . juice
jus d'orange . . . . orange juice
juste . . . . just, fair, right

<table>
<tr><td>K</td></tr>
</table>

kilo, le . . . . kilo
kilomètre, le . . . . kilometer
kiosque, le . . . . newstand

<table>
<tr><td>L</td></tr>
</table>

la, l', le, les . . . . the
lac, le . . . . lake
lait, le . . . . milk
laiterie, la . . . . dairy
lampe, la . . . . lamp
langage, le . . . . language
lavabo, le . . . . washbasin
laver . . . . to wash
leçon, la . . . . lesson
lecture, la . . . . reading
légume, le . . . . vegetable
lent (e) . . . . slow
lentement . . . . slowly
lettre, la . . . . letter
liberté, la . . . . liberty
librairie, la . . . . bookstore
libre . . . . free
lieu, le . . . . place
ligne, la . . . . line
limonade, la . . . . lemonade
linge, le . . . . linens
lingerie, la . . . . underclothing
lire . . . . to read
liste, la . . . . list
lit, le . . . . bed
wagon-lit, le . . . . sleeping car
litre, le . . . . liter
living-room, le . . . . living room

livre, le .... book
local (e) .... local
   appel téléphonique local, le ... local call
logement, le .... lodging
long, longue .... long
lorsque .... when
louer .... to rent
   voiture à louer, la .... rental car
lumière, la .... light
lundi, le .... Monday
lunettes, les .... glasses

M

Madame .... Mrs.
Mademoiselle .... Miss
magasin, le .... store
   grand magasin, le .... department store
magazine, le .... magazine
magnifique .... magnificent
mai, le .... May
maillot de bain, le .... swimsuit
main, la .... hand
   sac à main, le .... handbag
maintenant .... now
mais .... but
maison, la .... house
majorité, la .... majority
mal .... poorly, badly
   pas mal .... not too bad
malade .... sick
manger .... to eat
manteau, le .... coat
marchand, le .... merchant
marché, le .... market
   bon marché .... cheap, inexpensive
   marché aux puces .... flea market
mardi, le .... Tuesday
marron .... brown
mars, le .... March
matin, le .... morning
mauvais (e) .... bad
menu, le .... menu
mer, la .... sea
Mer du nord, la .... North Sea
merci .... thank you
mercredi, le .... Wednesday
mère, la .... mother
messieurs, les .... gentlemen
mètre, le .... meter
métro, métropolitain, le ... subway
meuble, le .... furniture
mieux .... better
mille .... one thousand
mince .... thin
minute, la .... minute
miroir, le .... mirror
mode, la .... fashion
   à la mode .... fashionable
moins .... less
   moins le quart .... a quarter to
mois, le .... month
moment, le .... moment
monde, le .... world
   tout le monde .... everyone
monnaie, la .... coins, money
montagne, la .... mountain
monter .... to board, climb
montre, la .... watch
montrer .... to show
mot, le .... word
mousse, la .... whipped cream, froth
moutarde, la .... mustard
mouton, le .... mutton
multicolore................ multi-colored
mur, le .... wall
musée, le .... museum
musulman (e) .... Moslem
musique, la .... music

N

nation, la .... nation
nature, la .... nature
ne ... pas, n' ... pas .... no, not
   n'est-ce pas? .... isn't it?
nécessaire .... necessary
nécessité, la .... necessity
neige (il neige) ...... snow (it is snowing)
neuf .... nine
neuf, neuve .... new
Noël .... Christmas
noir (e) .... black
nom, le .... name
nombre, le .... number
non .... no
nord, le .... north
normal (e) .... normal
Norvège, la .... Norway
note, la .... bill in hotel
nous .... we
nouveau, nouvelle .... new
novembre, le .... November
nuit, la .... night
numéro, le .... number

O

obligatoire .... compulsory
objet, le .... object
occupé (e) .... busy, occupied
odeur, la .... smell
oeuf, le .... egg
   oeuf mollet........... soft-boiled egg
   oeufs à la coque .... boiled eggs
   oeufs brouillés .... scrambled eggs
on .... one, people, they, we
   on fait ça .... one does that
   on dit que .... they say that
oncle, le .... uncle
ont/avoir .... have/to have
onze .... eleven
optimiste .... optimistic
orange, la .... orange
orchestre, le .... orchestra
ordinaire..................... ordinary
oreiller, le .... pillow
organisé (e) .... organized
Orient, le .... Orient
où .... where
ou .... or
oublier .... to forget
ouest, le .... west
oui .... yes
outil, le .... tool, implement
ouvert (e) .... open
ouvrez/ouvrir .... open/to open

P

page, la .... page
paiement, le .... payment
pain, le....................... bread
paire, la .... pair
pamplemousse, la .... grapefruit
pantalon, le .... pair of trousers
pantoufle, la................. slipper
papeterie, la .... stationery store
papier, le .... paper
papier-monnaie, le .... bills
paquet, le .... package
par .... by, per
par avion .... airmail
paragraphe, le .... paragraph
parapluie, le .... umbrella
parc, le .... park
pardon .... excuse me
parent, le .... parent, relative
parfait (e) .... perfect
   C'est parfait .... that's fine
parfumerie, la .... perfumery

parler....................... to speak
partir....................... to leave
pas bien .... not too well
pas mal .... not too badly
passe/passer .... happens/to happen
passeport, le .... passport
pâtisserie, la........ pastry, pastry shop
pauvre .... poor
payer....................... to pay
P.C.V. .... collect call
peigne, le .... comb
pellicule, la .... film
pelouse, la................... grass
pendule, la .... clock
perdre .... to lose
père, le .... father
personnes, les .... people
petit déjeuner, le .... breakfast
petit (e) .... small
peu .... little
peuple, le................... people
pharmacie, la .... pharmacy
photo, la .... photo, photograph
   appareil-photo, le .... camera
phrase, la .... sentence
pièce, la .... room, piece
pièce de monnaie, la .... coin
pied, le .... foot
pile, la .... battery
pilule, la .... pill
piscine, la .... pool
placard, le .... cupboard, closet
place, la .... seat, place
plafond, le .... ceiling
plage, la .... beach
plaisir, le .... pleasure
   avec plaisir .... with pleasure
plan, le .... map
pleut (il pleut) .... it is raining
plus .... more
pointure, la .... size (shoes and gloves)
poisson, le .... fish
poissonnerie, la .... fish market
poivre, le .... pepper
Pôle nord, le .... North Pole
Pôle sud, le .... South Pole
police, la .... police
politesse, la .... politeness
pomme, la .... apple
porc, le....................... pork
porte, la .... door
portefeuille, le .... wallet
poste, la .... mail
   bureau de poste, le .... post office
   P.T.T.................... post office
potage, le .... soup
pour .... for
pourboire, le .... tip
pourquoi .... why
pouvoir .... to be able to, can
pratique .... practical
premier, première .... first
préparer .... to prepare
préposition, la .... preposition
près d'ici .... near to here
printemps, le .... spring
prix, le .... price
problème, le .... problem
prochain (e) .... next
prolonger .... to lengthen
propre .... clean
protestant (e) .... Protestant
puis .... then
pyjama, le .... pajama

Q

quai, le....................... platform
quand....................... when

quarante . . . . forty
quart, le . . . . a quarter
   et quart . . . . a quarter past
   moins le quart . . . . a quarter to
quatorze . . . . fourteen
quatre . . . . four
quatre-vingt-dix . . . . ninety
quatre-vingts . . . . eighty
que, qu' . . . . what, that
qu'est-ce que c'est? . . . . what is it?
quel, quelle . . . . what, which
Quelle heure est-il? . . . . . What time is it?
question, la . . . . question
qui . . . . who, what
quincaillerie, la . . . . hardware store
quinze . . . . fifteen

R

radio, la . . . . radio
rasoir, le . . . . razor
rapide . . . . fast
Rapide, le (RAP) . . . . train
rapidement . . . . quickly
rayon, le . . . . department
récepteur, le . . . . receiver
recette, la . . . . recipe, receipt
réciter . . . . to recite
reçu, le . . . . receipt
réfrigérateur, le . . . . refrigerator
religion, la . . . . religion
renseignements, les . . . . information
   bureau de renseignements, le . . . .
. . . . information office
repas, le . . . . meal
répéter . . . . to repeat
répondre . . . . to reply, answer
réponse, la . . . . answer
rendez-vous, le . . . . . date, appointment
réservation, la . . . . reservation
réserver . . . . to reserve, to book
restaurant, le . . . . restaurant
restaurant routier, le . . . . truck stop
reste, le . . . . rest, remaining
rester . . . . to remain, stay
retard, le . . . . delay
   en retard . . . . late
réveil, le . . . . alarm clock
revue, la . . . . magazine
rez-de-chaussée, le . . . . ground floor
riche . . . . rich
rideau, le . . . . curtain
rien . . . . nothing
robe, la . . . . dress
robe de chambre, la . . . . bathrobe
rose . . . . pink
rose, la . . . . rose
rôti (e) . . . . roasted
rouge . . . . red
route, la . . . . road
rue, la . . . . street
russe . . . . Russian

S

sac, le . . . . bag, sack
   sac à main, le . . . . handbag
saison, la . . . . season
salade, la . . . . salad
salle à manger, la . . . . dining room
salle d'attente, la . . . . waiting room
salle de bain, la . . . . bathroom
salut . . . . hi
salutations, les . . . . greetings
samedi, le . . . . Saturday
sandale, la . . . . sandal
sang, le . . . . blood
santé, la . . . . healthy
saucisse, la . . . . sausage
saucisson, le . . . . salami, sausage
savoir . . . . to know (a fact)

savon, le . . . . soap
second (e) . . . . second
seize . . . . sixteen
sel, le . . . . salt
semaine, la . . . . week
sept . . . . seven
septembre, le . . . . September
serveur, le . . . . waiter
serveuse, la . . . . waitress
service, le . . . . service
serviette, la . . . . napkin, towel
   grande serviette, la . . . . large towel
seulement . . . . only
signalisations, les . . . . signs
s'il vous plaît . . . . please
similarité, la . . . . similarity
simple . . . . simple, single, ordinary
six . . . . six
slip, le . . . . underpants
SNCF . . . . French national railroad
soeur, la . . . . sister
soir, le . . . . evening
soixante . . . . sixty
soixante-dix . . . . seventy
soleil, le . . . . sun
somme, la . . . . sum
sonnette, la . . . . doorbell
sont/être . . . . are/to be
sortie, la . . . . exit
   sortie de secours, la . . . . emergency exit
   sortie principale, la . . . . main exit
sortir . . . . to go out
soulier, le . . . . shoe
soupe, la . . . . soup
sous . . . . under
sous-sol, le . . . . basement
soutien-gorge, le . . . . brassiere
souvenir, le . . . . souvenir
souvent . . . . often
specialité de la maison, la . . . .
. . . . specialty of the house
sport, le . . . . sport
standardiste, le . . . . operator
station d'essence, la . . . . gas station
stopper . . . . to stop
stylo, le . . . . pen
sucre, le . . . . sugar
sud, le . . . . south
Suède, la . . . . Sweden
suis/être . . . . am/to be
Suisse, la . . . . Switzerland
suivant (e) . . . . following
supérieur (e) . . . . superior, upper
supermarché, le . . . . supermarket
sur . . . . on
sympathique . . . . likeable, nice
système, le . . . . system

T

tabac, le . . . . tobacco
table, la . . . . table
tableau, le . . . . picture
taille, la . . . . size (clothing)
tailleur, le . . . . tailor
tante, la . . . . aunt
tapis, le . . . . carpet
tapisserie, la . . . . tapestry, wallpaper
tarte, la . . . . pie
tarte aux pommes, la . . . . apple pie
taxe, la . . . . tax, charge
taxi, le . . . . taxi
télégramme, le . . . . telegram
téléphone, le . . . . telephone
téléphoner . . . . to telephone
téléphoniste, le . . . . operator
téléviseur, le . . . . television set
température, la . . . . temperature
temps, le . . . . weather, time
terrasse, la . . . . terrace, sidewalk

tête, la . . . . head
thé, le . . . . tea
théâtre, le . . . . theater
thermomètre, le . . . . thermometer
ticket, le . . . . ticket
timbre-poste, le . . . . stamp
toilettes, les . . . . toilets
tour, la . . . . tower
tourner . . . . to turn
tout droit . . . . straight ahead
train, le . . . . train
transport, le . . . . transportation
treize . . . . thirteen
trente . . . . thirty
très . . . . very
trois . . . . three
troisième . . . . third
trouver . . . . to find
typique . . . . typical

U

un (e) . . . . a, one
unique . . . . sole, only, single

V

vacances, les . . . . vacation, holiday
vais/aller . . . . go/to go
vaisselle, la . . . . dishes
valise, la . . . . suitcase
vanille, la . . . . vanilla
variété, la . . . . variety
veau, le . . . . veal, calf
vendre . . . . to sell
venir . . . . to come
vent, le . . . . wind
vente, la . . . . sale
verbe, le . . . . verb
verre, le . . . . glass
vert (e) . . . . green
veston, le . . . . man's jacket
vêtement, le . . . . clothes
veuillez . . . . would you please
viande, la . . . . meat
vie, la . . . . life
vient/venir . . . . comes/to come
vierge, la . . . . virgin
vieux, vieille . . . . old
vigne, la . . . . grape vine
ville, la . . . . city
vin, le . . . . wine
vingt . . . . twenty
violet/violette . . . . violet
visite, la . . . . visit
vite . . . . fast
vocabulaire, le . . . . vocabulary
voie, la . . . . track
voilà . . . . there is/there are
voir . . . . to see
voiture, la . . . . car
   voiture à louer, la . . . . rental car
volaille, la . . . . poultry
votre . . . . your
voudrais . . . . I would like
voudrions . . . . we would like
vouloir . . . . to want
vous . . . . you
voyage, le . . . . trip, travel
   agence de voyage, la . . . . . travel agency
   Bon voyage! . . . . have a good trip
voyageur, le . . . . traveler

W

wagon, le . . . . railroad car
wagon-lit, le . . . . sleeping car
wagon-restaurant, le . . . . dining car
W. C., les . . . . water closet, toilet

Y

y a-t-il . . . . are there/is there?

111

DRINKING GUIDE

This guide is intended to explain the sometimes overwhelming variety of beverages available to you while in France. It is by no means complete. Some of the experimenting has been left up to you, but this should get you started. The asterisks (*) indicate brand names.

BOISSONS CHAUDES (hot drinks)

café noir	coffee, black
café au lait	coffee with milk
café crème	coffee with cream
café express	expresso
café filtre	filtered coffee
thé	tea
au citron	with lemon
au lait	with milk
chocolat	hot chocolate

BOISSONS FROIDES (cold drinks)

lait froid	cold milk
lait aromatisé	flavored milk
eau minérale	mineral water
*Vittel	
*Perrier	
*Vichy	
limonade	lemonade
jus de fruits	fruit juice
jus d'orange	orange juice
jus de pomme	apple juice
jus de tomate	tomato juice
orange pressé	squeezed orange juice
citron pressé	squeezed lemon juice
cidre	cider
thé glacé	iced tea
café glacé	iced coffee

APÉRITIFS (aperitifs) These may be enjoyed straight or over ice.

porto	port
xérès	sherry
Pineau de Charente	grape juice and cognac
Kir	Crème de Cassis and white wine

*Pernod/Pastis/Ricard	anise base
*Campari	*Martini blanc
*Cinzano	*Martini rouge
*Dubonnet	*St. Raphaël

COGNAC (cognac) Cognac is a special type of brandy and is only produced in the region of Cognac.

*Rémy Martin	*St. Rémy
*Courvoisier	*Martell
*Hennessy	*Hine

CHAMPAGNE (champagne) Champagne only comes from the region of Champagne.

*Dom Perignon (the monk who invented champagne)
*Mumms
*Piper-Heidsieck
*Taitinger
*Moët et Chandon
*Bollinger

  **LA GLACE** .... ice

BIÈRES (beers) There are a variety of brands including both **blonde** (light) and **brune** (dark). **La bière** is purchased in **bouteille** (bottle) or **à la pression** (draught).

PRESSION (draught)

*Kronenbourg Export

le demi	small glass
le baron	medium glass
la chope	tankard

BOUTEILLE (bottle)

*Kanterbrau
*Kronenbourg
*Pelforth brune
*Tuborg
*Paulaner

VINS (wines) The wine production in France is closely controlled by the government, making it much easier to know what you are buying. You may drink wine by the **verre** (glass), the **carafe** (carafe) or the **bouteille** (bottle).

vin rouge	red wine
vin blanc	white wine
vin rosé	rosé wine
vin mousseux	sparkling wine
vin ordinaire	table wine
vin de table	table wine
vin de la maison	the "house" wine
vin du pays	local wine of the region

A.O.C. (Appelation d'origine contrôlée)
superior wine
V.D.Q.S. (Vins délimités de qualité supérieure)
choice wine
Premier cru/Grand cru
good vintage wine

The major wine-producing areas **de la France** are

Bordeaux	Bourgogne
Loire	Côtes du Rhône
Alsace	Champagne

ALCOOL (spirits) Cocktail drinking is not wide-spread in France. The following are available in large, international hotels and "Bars américains."

gin	gin
vodka	vodka
rhum	rum
whiskey	scotch
bourbon	bourbon
martini dry	American martini

DIGESTIFS (liqueurs, brandies)

eau de vie	grain natural spirits
fine à l'eau	brandy and soda
*Drambuie	*Armagnac
*Cointreau	*Chartreuse
*Grand Marnier	*Bénédictine

La Carte

FOLD HERE

Préparation (preparation)

cuit	cooked
cru	raw
rôti	roasted
frit	fried
cuit au four	baked
grillé	grilled
farci/fourré	stuffed or filled
bouilli	boiled
fumé	smoked
mariné	marinated
braisé	braised
en croûte	cooked in crust
en cocotte	cooked in earthenware
au gratin	sprinkled with cheese
au lard	cooked in salt pork
au jus	cooked in its own juice
bleu	extremely rare
saignant	rare
à point	medium rare
bien cuit	well done

Autres (others)

confiture	jam
miel	honey
sel	salt
poivre	pepper
huile	oil
vinaigre	vinegar
moutarde	mustard
riz	rice
pain	bread
baguette	long loaf of bread
nouilles	noodles
pâtes	pasta
fromage	cheese
dessert	dessert
gâteau	cake
pâtisserie	pastry
glace	ice cream
chantilly	whipped cream
yaourt	yoghurt

Pommes de terre (potatoes)

croquettes	mashed, dipped and fried
gratin dauphinois	scalloped
frites	French fried
à l'anglaise	peeled and boiled
nature	plain boiled
maître d'hôtel	boiled and sautéed
purée	mashed
vapeur	steamed

Fruit (fruit)

pomme	apple
poire	pear
abricot	apricot
pêche	peach
banane	banana
orange	orange
mandarine	mandarin orange
cerise	cherry
prune	plum
pruneau	prune
melon	melon
pamplemousse	grapefruit
pastèque	watermelon
raisin	grape
raisin sec	raisin
grenade	pomegranate
ananas	pineapple
citron	lemon
compote de fruits	stewed fruits

Baies (berries)

fraise	strawberry
framboise	raspberry
mûre	blackberry
groseille à maquereau	gooseberry
groseille (rouge, blanche)	red or white currant
cassis	black currant
myrtille	bilberry
airelle	blueberry

Bon appétit!

Salades (salads)

laitue	lettuce salad
laitue chicorée	chicory
escarole	coarse-leafed green lettuce
endive belge	Belgian endive
mâche	wild field lettuce
romaine	romaine
mélangée	mixed
mimosa	green salad with egg yolks
mixte	mixed
niçoise	string beans, potatoes, tuna
verte	tossed green
de pissenlits	dandelion greens
de saison	seasonal
de tomates	tomato
vinaigrette	in vinegar and oil

Légumes (vegetables)

haricots verts	green string beans
haricots flageolets	small, pale green beans
petits pois	peas
lentilles	lentils
asperges	asparagus
carottes	carrots
épinards	spinach
poireaux	leeks
tomates	tomatoes
champignons	cultivated mushrooms
chanterelles	wild mushrooms
morilles	morel, wild mushrooms
chou	cabbage
chou-fleur	cauliflower
choux de Bruxelles	brussels sprouts
betteraves	beets
maïs	corn
concombres	cucumbers
navets	turnips
oignons	onions
radis	radishes
ail	garlic
artichauts	artichoke
aubergines	eggplant
courgettes	zucchini squash
macédoine des légumes	diced, cooked vegetables

FOLD HERE

Hors-d'oeuvre (hors-d'oeuvres)

huîtres	oysters
assiette de charcuterie	assorted sausages, salamis
céleri-rave rémoulade	celery root in sauce
coeur de palmier	hearts of palm
crudités	raw vegetables
escargots	snails
foie gras truffé	goose liver with truffles
jambon cru	raw-cured ham
langue de boeuf gelée	beef tongue with aspic
pâté de campagne	country style, course paté
salade panachée	mixed vegetable salad
saucisson	sausage/salami
terrine maison	house paté in terrine
croque monsieur	grilled ham and cheese sandwich
croque madame	grilled chicken and cheese sandwich

Potages, soupes (soups)

bisque	cream soup with seafood
bouillabaisse	rich fish soup
crème de tomates	cream of tomato
petite marmite	soup-stew
pistou	vegetable soup
soupe du jour	soup of the day
soupe à l'oignon	onion soup
consommé	clarified stock
soupe à la reine	chicken soup with rice
velouté de légumes	thick vegetable soup
vichyssoise	potato and leek soup

Oeufs (eggs)

à la coque	soft-boiled
mollet	medium-boiled
brouillés	scrambled
dur	hard-boiled
poché	poached
omelette nature	plain omelette
omelette au fromage	cheese omelette
quiche	cheese and egg pie
... à cheval	... topped with a fried egg
au plat	fried (sometimes baked)

Viande (meat)

Veau (veal)

blanquette de veau	veal stew with gravy
côte de veau	veal chop
côtelette de veau	veal chop
foie de veau	calf's liver

Viande (meat) — continued

fricassée de veau	veal stew
jarret de veau	veal shank
médaillons de veau	discs of pan-fried veal
noisette de veau	tenderloin morsels of veal
poitrine de veau farcie	stuffed breast of veal
ris de veau	veal sweetbreads
rognons de veau	veal kidneys
rôti de veau	roast veal
tendron de veau	braised breast of veal
tête de veau	head of veal
escalope de veau	veal cutlet

Boeuf (beef)

boeuf bourguignon	red wine stew
carbonades de boeuf	sautéed and braised slices
côte de boeuf	beef rib steaks
daube de boeuf	marinated pot-roast
entrecôte de boeuf	boneless beef rib steak
estouffade de boeuf	braised beef in wine stew
filet de boeuf	tenderloin of beef
langue de boeuf	beef tongue
médaillon de boeuf	thick discs of tenderloin
queue de boeuf	oxtail
braisé de boeuf	beef stew in wine
tournedos	beef tenderloin
terrine de boeuf	casserole stew
tripes	stomach lining
moelle	beef bone marrow

Porc (pork)

côte/côtelette de porc	pork chop
carré de porc provençal	rib loin roast with spices
cuissot de porc	fresh ham roast
jarret de porc	pork shank
noisette de porc	small tenderloin discs
pied de porc	pig's foot
rognons de porc	pork kidneys
rôti de porc	pork roast
tête de porc roulée	rolled pig's head
cochon au lait	suckling pig (roasted)

Agneau (lamb)

carré d'agneau	lamb rib roast
côte/côtelette d'agneau	lamb chop
épaule d'agneau	lamb shoulder
gigot d'agneau	leg of lamb
cervelle d'agneau	lamb's brains

Volaille (poultry)

poulet	chicken
coq au vin	chicken in wine sauce
canard	duck
caneton	duckling
chapon	capon
caille	quail
oie	goose
faisan	pheasant
pigeon	pigeon
dinde	turkey

Gibier (wild game)

gigue de chevreuil	roast leg of venison
bécasse	woodcock
escalope de sanglier	cutlets of wild boar
cuissot de marcassin	roast leg of wild pig
râble de lapin	saddle of rabbit
lapin sauté chasseur	rabbit sautéed in wine

Poissons et fruits de mer (fish and seafood)

anchois	anchovies
anguille	eel
cabillaud	codfish
calamar	squid
carpe	carp
colin	hake
coquillages	shellfish
coquilles Saint-Jacques	scallops
crabe	crab
crevettes	shrimps
écrevisses	fresh-water crayfish
flétan	halibut
grenouille	frog
hareng	herring
homard	true lobster, with claws
langouste	spiny lobster; no claws
langoustine	
morue	dried codfish
moules	mussels
oursins	sea urchins
perche	perch
poulpe	small octopus
quenelles	cylindrical fish dumpling
rouget de roche	Mediterranean red mullet
saumon	salmon
sole	sole
truite	trout
thon	tuna

(vuh-neer)
venir

(saw-puh-lay)
s'appeler

(ah-lay)
aller

(ah-shuh-tay)
acheter

(ah-vwahr)
avoir

(par-lay)
parler

(ah-prah⁽ⁿ⁾-druh)
apprendre

(ah-bee-tay)
habiter

(zhuh) *(voo-dray)*
je voudrais

(ko-mah⁽ⁿ⁾-day)
commander

(ah-vwahr) *(buh-zwa⁽ⁿ⁾)* *(duh)*
avoir besoin de

(reh-stay)
rester

to be called	to come
to buy	to go
to speak	to have
to live/reside	to learn
to order	I would like
to stay/remain	to need

(deer) **dire**	*(vah[n]-druh)* **vendre**
(mah[n]-zhay) **manger**	*(vwahr)* **voir**
(bwahr) **boire**	*(ah[n]-vwhy-ay)* **envoyer**
(ah-tah[n]-druh) **attendre**	*(door-meer)* **dormir**
(koh[n]-prah[n]-druh) **comprendre**	*(troo-vay)* **trouver**
(ray-pay-tay) **répéter**	*(fare)* **faire**

to sell	to say
to see	to eat
to send	to drink
to sleep	to wait
to find	to understand
to do/make	to repeat

(ay-kreer)
écrire

(leer)
lire

(moh(n)-tray)
montrer

(vwhy-ah-zhay)
voyager

(pay-yay)
payer

(trah-vhy-ay)
travailler

(poo-vwahr)
pouvoir

(prah(n)-druh) *(lah-vee-oh(n))*
prendre l'avion

(duh-vwahr)
devoir

(eel) *(foh)*
il faut

(sah-vwahr)
savoir

(fare) *(vah-leez)*
fair la valise

to read	to write
to travel	to show
to work	to pay
to fly	to be able to/can
it is necessary	to have to/must/owe
to pack	to know

(koh-mah(n)-say)
commencer

(prah(n)-druh)
prendre

(oov-rear)
ouvrir

(moh(n)-tay)
monter

(fare) *(kwee-zeen)*
faire la cuisine

(day-sah(n)-druh)
descendre

(ah-tair-ear)
atterrir

(day-bar-kay)
débarquer

(ray-zair-vay)
réserver

(shah(n)-zhay) *(duh)*
changer de . . .

(koo-tay)
coûter

(ah-ree-vay)
arriver

to take	to begin
to climb/board	to open
to go down/get out	to cook
to disembark	to land
to transfer	to book/reserve
to arrive	to cost

(par-teer)
partir

(fair-may)
fermer

(koh(n)-dweer)
conduire

(lah-vay)
laver

(few-may)
fumer

(shah(n)-zhay)
changer

(duh-mah(n)-day)
demander

(pair-druh)
perdre

(eel) *(nehzh)*
il neige

(zhuh) *(swee)*
je suis

(eel) *(pluh)*
il pleut

(new) *(sohm)*
nous sommes

to close	to depart/leave
to wash	to drive
to exchange	to smoke
to lose	to ask
I am	it is snowing
we are	it is raining

(eel)
il
(ell)
elle } *(ay)* **est**

(oh) *(bah)*
haut - bas

(voo-zet)
vous êtes

(poh-vruh) *(reesh)*
pauvre - riche

(eel)
il
(ell)
elle } *(soh$^{(n)}$)* **sont**

(koor) *(loh$^{(n)}$)*
court - long

(oh) *(ruh-vwahr)*
au revoir

(mah-lahd)
malade -
(ah$^{(n)}$) *(bun)* *(form)*
en bonne forme

(eel-ee-ah)
il y a

(boh$^{(n)}$) *(mar-shay)* *(share)*
bon marché - cher

(ko-mah$^{(n)}$) *(tah-lay-voo)*
Comment allez-vous?

(vee-yuh) *(zhun)*
vieux - jeune

high - low

he
she   is

poor - rich

you are

short - long

they are

sick - healthy

good-bye

cheap - expensive

there is/there are

old - young

How are you?

bon - mauvais
(boh[n]) *(mow-vay)*

vite/rapide - lent
(veet) *(rah-peed)* *(lah[n])*

doucement - fort
(deuce-mah[n]) *(for)*

gros - mince
(grow) *(ma[n]s)*

grand - petite
(grah[n]) *(puh-tee)*

beaucoup de - peu de
(boh-koo) *(duh)* *(puh)* *(duh)*

chaud - froid
(show) *(fwah)*

ouvert - fermé
(oo-vair) *(fair-may)*

gauche - droit
(gohsh) *(dwah)*

doux - aigre
(doo) *(ay-gruh)*

en haut - en bas
(ah[n]) *(oh)* *(ah[n])* *(bas)*

excusez-moi/pardon
(ek-skew-zay-mwah) *(par-doh[n])*

fast - slow

good - bad

thick - thin

soft - loud

much - little

large - small

open - closed

warm - cold

sweet - sour

left - right

excuse me

above - below